REGENTS RENAISSANCE DRAMA SERIES

*General Editor:* Cyrus Hoy
*Advisory Editor:* G. E. Bentley

# THE REVENGER'S TRAGEDY

CYRIL TOURNEUR

# The Revenger's Tragedy

*Edited by*

LAWRENCE J. ROSS

UNIVERSITY OF NEBRASKA PRESS · LINCOLN

MANUFACTURED IN THE UNITED STATES OF AMERICA

# Regents Renaissance Drama Series

The purpose of the Regents Renaissance Drama Series is to provide soundly edited texts, in modern spelling, of the more significant plays of the Elizabethan, Jacobean, and Caroline theater. Each text in the series is based on a fresh collation of all sixteenth- and seventeenth-century editions. The textual notes, which appear above the line at the bottom of each page, record all substantive departures from the edition used as the copy-text. Variant substantive readings among sixteenth- and seventeenth-century editions are listed there as well. In cases where two or more of the old editions present widely divergent readings, a list of substantive variants in editions through the seventeenth century is given in an appendix. Editions after 1700 are referred to in the textual notes only when an emendation originating in some one of them is received into the text. Variants of accidentals (spelling, punctuation, capitalization) are not recorded in the notes. Contracted forms of characters' names are silently expanded in speech prefixes and stage directions, and, in the case of speech prefixes, are regularized. Additions to the stage directions of the copy-text are enclosed in brackets. Stage directions such as "within" or "aside" are enclosed in parentheses when they occur in the copy-text.

Spelling has been modernized along consciously conservative lines. "Murther" has become "murder," and "burthen," "burden," but within the limits of a modernized text, and with the following exceptions, the linguistic quality of the original has been carefully preserved. The variety of contracted forms (*'em*, *'am*, *'m*, *'um*, *'hem*) used in the drama of the period for the pronoun *them* are here regularly given as *'em*, and the alternation between *a'th'* and *o'th'* (for *on* or *of the*) is regularly reproduced as *o'th'*. The copy-text distinction between preterite endings in *-d* and *-ed* is preserved except where the elision of *e* occurs in the penultimate syllable; in such cases, the final syllable is contracted. Thus, where the old editions read "threat'ned," those of the present series read "threaten'd." Where, in the old editions, a contracted preterite in *-y'd* would yield *-i'd* in modern spelling (as in "try'd," "cry'd," "deny'd"), the word is here given in its full form (e.g., "tried," "cried," "denied").

Punctuation has been brought into accord with modern practices. The effort here has been to achieve a balance between the generally light pointing of the old editions, and a system of punctuation which, without overloading the text with exclamation marks, semicolons, and dashes, will make the often loosely flowing verse (and prose) of the original syntactically intelligible to the modern reader. Dashes are regularly used only to indicate interrupted speeches, or shifts of address within a single speech.

Explanatory notes, chiefly concerned with glossing obsolete words and phrases, are printed below the textual notes at the bottom of each page. References to stage directions in the notes follow the admirable system of the Revels editions, whereby stage directions are keyed, decimally, to the line of the text before or after which they occur. Thus, a note on 0.2 has reference to the second line of the stage direction at the beginning of the scene in question. A note on 115.1 has reference to the first line of the stage direction following line 115 of the text of the relevant scene.

CYRUS HOY

University of Rochester

# Acknowledgments

The present edition is the result of a new collation of nine exemplars of the 1607–1608 quarto and a fresh, intensive study of the play; but I of course owe a debt to former editors and students far greater than my notes can possibly suggest.

I am also deeply indebted for other kinds of aid: to the Washington University Faculty Research Committee for a grant which enabled purchase of some of the requisite xerox prints and preparation of the final copy; and to the Folger Shakespeare Library, and its Director, Dr. Louis B. Wright, for a Fellowship during the summer of 1964, partially devoted, with the aid of its fine staff, to work on this edition among its splendid resources and happy company. I should also like to express my appreciation for the unfailing courtesy of the other libraries cited in the section on the text, and for their permission to study their exemplars of the quarto either in the original or xerox.

My wife has helped in the proof-reading, for which I am thankful; for her supportive interest and unending patience, there is only my love.

L. J. R.

# Contents

# List of Abbreviations

Bailey N. Bailey. *An Universal Etymological English Dictionary.* 9th ed. London, 1740.

Collier Gilchrist J. P. Collier, *et al.*, eds. Dodsley's *A Select Collection of Old Plays.* London, 1825. Vol. IV.

Collins John Churton Collins, ed. *The Plays and Poems of Cyril Tourneur.* London, 1878. Vol. II.

conj. conjecture

corr. corrected

Cotgrave Randle Cotgrave. *A Dictionarie of the French and English Tongues.* London, 1611 (facsimile: Columbia, S.C., 1950).

Dodsley Robert Dodsley, ed. *A Select Collection of Old Plays.* London, 1744. Vol. IV.

*EIC* *Essays in Criticism*

*ELH* *ELH: A Journal of English Literary History*

Florio John Florio. *A Worlde of Wordes.* London, 1598.

Grose Francis Grose. *A Classical Dictionary of the Vulgar Tongue* [1785], ed. Eric Partridge. 3rd ed. (reprinted London, 1963).

Harrier Richard C. Harrier, ed. *An Anthology of Jacobean Drama.* New York, 1963. Vol. II.

Harrison G. B. Harrison, ed. *The Revenger's Tragedy.* (The Temple Dramatists.) London, 1934.

Hazlitt W. Carew Hazlitt, ed. Dodsley's *A Select Collection of Old Plays.* London, 1876. Vol. X.

Mermaid Symonds *John Webster and Cyril Tourneur.* (Mermaid ed.) With an introduction and notes by John Addington Symonds. London, 1888.

*MLR* *Modern Language Review*

| | |
|---|---|
| Napier | C. S. Napier. "The Revenger's Tragedy," *London Times Literary Supplement*, March 13, 1937, p. 188. |
| Nares | Robert Nares. *A Glossary; or, Collection of Words, Phrases, Names, and Allusions to Customs, Proverbs, &c. which have been thought to require Illustration, in the works of English Authors, particularly Shakespeare, and his Contemporaries.* London, 1822. |
| Nicoll | Allardyce Nicoll, ed. *The Works of Cyril Tourneur.* [1929], reprinted New York, 1963. |
| *N & Q* | *Notes and Queries* |
| *OED* | *Oxford English Dictionary* |
| Onions | C. T. Onions. *A Shakespeare Glossary.* 2nd ed. rev. Oxford, 1949. |
| Panofsky | Erwin Panofsky. *Studies in Iconology.* New York, 1939. |
| Partridge | Eric Partridge. *Shakespeare's Bawdy.* New York, 1948. |
| *PMLA* | *Publications of the Modern Language Association of America* |
| *Q* | The 1607–1608 quarto of *The Revenger's Tragedy* |
| Reed Johnson Pegge Steevens | Isaac Reed, ed. Dodsley's *A Select Collection of Old Plays.* London, 1780. Vol. IV. (With cited annotations by Samuel Johnson, Samuel Pegge, and George Steevens.) |
| *RES* | *Review of English Studies* |
| Salingar | L. G. Salingar. "Tourneur and the Tragedy of Revenge," in *The Age of Shakespeare.* Penguin Books, 1955. |
| S.D. | stage direction |
| S.P. | speech prefix |
| Swinburne | Algernon Charles Swinburne. *The Age of Shakespeare.* London, 1908. |
| Tilley | Morris Palmer Tilley. *A Dictionary of the Proverbs in England in the Sixteenth and Seventeenth Centuries.* Ann Arbor, 1950. |
| uncorr. | uncorrected |

The following editions have been consulted but not cited in notes: [Sir Walter Scott, supposed ed.] *Ancient British Drama*, London, 1810, Vol. II; Ashley H. Thorndike, ed., *Elizabethan Minor Dramatists*, New York, 1916; E. H. C. Oliphant, ed., *Shakespeare and His Fellow*

*Dramatists*, New York, 1929; G. H. W. Rylands, ed., *Elizabethan Tragedy: Six Representative Plays*, London, 1933; Henri Fluchère, ed., *La Tragédie du Vengeur*, Paris, 1960; *The Revenger's Tragedy* (Chandler Editions: Robert W. Corrigan, ed.), San Francisco, 1962.

□                                                    □

# Introduction

On October 7, 1607, an unusual double entry was made in the
Register of the Stationers' Company, the copyright book of London
publishers. George Eld

> Entred for his copies vnder th[e h]andes of Sir George Buck and
> th[e] wardens. Twoo plaies th[e] one called *the revengers tragedie*
> th[e] other. *A trick to catche the old one*. . . . xij<sup>d1</sup>

Eld soon published the former play in quarto; since a variant of the
edition alters the date from 1607 to 1608, it is probable the printing
occurred late in Old Style 1607. The title page reads as follows:

> THE REVENGERS TRAGÆDIE./ *As it hath beene sundry times
> Acted,/ by the Kings Maiesties/ Seruants./* [Ornament]/ AT
> LONDON/ Printed by G. Eld, and are to be sold at his house
> in Fleete-lane at the signe of the/ Printers-Presse./ 1607.

No contemporary allusion to the play or reference (other than that
on the title page) to its early stage history is known to survive. The
corruption in the text at IV.iv.14 may be due to the compositor's
difficulty with a line altered to conform with the ordinance against
profanity of May 27, 1606, but it does not necessarily follow that the
play already existed before that date.[2] The Stationers' Register entry
thus provides our only reliable latter terminus in dating. A date
before which the play is unlikely to have been written is determined
by its dependence on Marston's satiric comedies, *The Malcontent*
(perhaps 1602–1603), and *The Fawn* (between 1604 and 1606), its
echoing of *King Lear* (1605), and the clear influence on it of Jonson's

---

[1] Edward Arber, ed., *A Transcript of the Registers of the Company of Stationers
of London*, III (London, 1876), 360.

[2] George R. Price, "The Authorship and the Bibliography of *The
Revenger's Tragedy*," *The Library*, 5th Ser., XV (1960), 270, assumes it
probably does. But see W. W. Greg, *The Shakespeare First Folio* (Oxford,
1955), p. 152.

*Volpone* (probably acted early 1606, New Style).[3] *The Revenger's Tragedy* reasonably may be supposed, therefore, to have been written sometime between spring, 1606, and the entry in 1607.

This major poetic drama, anonymous in its original publication, yet remains the most important play of the surviving Elizabethan repertory to have its authorship in dispute. The weakness of our basic external evidence has invited controversy. The earliest documentary attributions are found in the play lists after the closing of the theaters: that of Edward Archer (appended to *The Old Law*, 1656), in which the tragedy is attributed to "*Tournour*," and those of Francis Kirkman (appended to *Tom Tyler*, 1661, and *Nicomede*, 1671), in which the author is claimed to be "*Cyrill Tourneur*."[4] The testimony of these often unreliable lists, though relatively early, is far from unassailable; yet it should immediately be emphasized that the tendency in their many erroneous attributions is to award authorship to noted figures, not minor ones like Tourneur.[5] But we have no way of knowing the adequacy of the grounds on which this particular attribution was made. Consistency in theme, moral tone, and imagery between the play and *The Transformed Metamorphosis*, an obscure allegoric verse satire on religion published by Tourneur in 1600, make the assignment to him initially not implausible. However, in the absence of other, determinate, external evidence, and with one eye on the differences in style and apparent intellectual posture between this play and *The Atheist's Tragedy* (the only one extant attributed on its title page to Cyril Tourneur), a number of modern scholars have pressed the candidacy of other playwrights for the authorship, principally Marston, Webster, and Middleton.

Thomas Middleton has been the most frequent and convincing contender, though it must be noted that nothing more than mere speculation ever has been offered to explain how a principal writer for boy actors, at this date engaged in writing city comedies for private theater performance, should have been responsible for a revenge

[3] This date for *The Malcontent*, variously set between 1600 and 1604, is that preferred by Antoni Caputi, *John Marston, Satirist* (Ithaca, 1961), pp. 265–266 and by M. L. Wine, editor of the play for this series (1964). For the other dates, see E. K. Chambers, *The Elizabethan Stage* (Oxford, 1933), III, 432, 368; IV, 42.

[4] W. W. Greg, *A Bibliography of the English Printed Drama to the Restoration*, III (London, 1957), 1336, 1350.

[5] See S. Schoenbaum, "Internal Evidence and the Attribution of Elizabethan Plays," *Bulletin of the New York Public Library*, LXV (1961), 121.

tragedy produced—as the title page asserts and the staging called for in the text confirms—by the King's Men, and undoubtedly at the Globe.[6] Neither is it at all clear that the joint entry of the play in the Stationers' Register with one unquestionably by Middleton has any significance for the question of authorship.[7] The controversy over the claims of Tourneur and Middleton, which has already lasted half a century and been productive of a voluminous literature, has rested perforce on comparative study of various kinds of internal evidence. This exasperatingly protracted argument has not conclusively established either playwright as the certain author, and it may not be capable of doing so. Indeed, its main usefulness may prove to have been the impetus it has given to intensive critical study of the play and the two dramatists, and to refinement and reassessment of the use of internal evidence in studies of attribution.[8]

Considerations of space permit only the barest summary discussion here of the various and complex arguments from internal evidence which have figured in this controversy.[9] Each involves special difficulties. All have been bedeviled by a radical limitation in the raw materials from which evidence might be drawn. The plays of the two authors available for comparison are either unsuitable as to kind, or insufficient in number, or too distant from *The Revenger's Tragedy* in time or by virtue of possibly substantial authorial development. For Tourneur we have only the uncontested *The Atheist's*

[6] *Ibid.*; and Inga-Stina Ekeblad, "A Note on 'The Revenger's Tragedy,'" *N & Q*, CC (1955), 98. Since Harold N. Hillebrand's "Thomas Middleton's *The Viper's Brood*," *Modern Language Notes*, XLII (1927), 35–38, others have repeated his attempt to identify *The Revenger's Tragedy* with *The Viper and Her Brood*, a play not extant which Middleton claimed, in a lawsuit, to have been delivered to impresario Robert Keysar in partial payment of a debt in June, 1606. Excellent reasons for supposing *The Viper's Brood* a mare's nest in this attribution problem are offered by R. A. Foakes, "On the Authorship of *The Revenger's Tragedy*," *MLR*, XLVIII (1953), 135–136.

[7] Peter B. Murray, *A Study of Cyril Tourneur* (Philadelphia, 1964), pp. 145–146, argues that it may.

[8] See Schoenbaum, "Internal Evidence"; also G. E. Bentley, "Authenticity and Attribution in the Jacobean and Caroline Drama," *English Institute Annual 1942* (New York, 1943), pp. 101–118.

[9] The first detailed case for Middleton was presented by E. H. C. Oliphant, "The Authorship of *The Revenger's Tragedy*," *Studies in Philology*, XXIII (1926), 157–168. The controversy to 1954 is summarized in Samuel Schoenbaum, *Middleton's Tragedies: A Critical Study* (New York, 1955), pp. 153–182; to 1961 in Murray, pp. 144–159.

*Tragedy* (published 1611); Middleton's surviving plays for the years 1602–1609 are all comedies and his great tragic plays, *Women Beware Women* and *The Changeling*, were written fifteen years after the drama in question. Furthermore, *The Revenger's Tragedy*, although scarcely to be considered apart from the various conventions and traditions it richly fuses, is in certain respects a unique play, and therefore unlike either Tourneur or Middleton;[10] we look in vain in the writings of either before 1606 for anything approaching this play's depth, organic brilliance, and intricate metaphoric texture.

Scholars arguing from internal evidence have been constrained to deal in parallels: in moral or philosophic position, theme, use of convention, dramatic technique, characterization, imagery, versification, and expression. Any and all of this remains indeterminate since little thus proffered as evidence of authorship cannot readily be construed to be due to imitation, influence, or shared convention. The parallelism between this play and *The Atheist's Tragedy*—in concern, moral emphasis, symbolism, imagery, methods of characterization, use of revenge play conventions, ironic structuring of action, predilection for allegory, and so on—seems impressive despite the patently substantial differences in style, until we realize that none of it is sufficiently peculiar to Tourneur to serve as indisputable evidence of authorship. Even after we subtract the levyings upon common stock, the weight of parallelism in phrase would seem to point to Middleton; yet no responsible modern scholar will neglect to observe that the method permits no distinction between imitation or conventional expression and common authorship.

Other arguments have foundered in the uncertain seas of interpretation. In those focusing on versification the difficulties begin even with the requisite data. Since there clearly is a good deal of mislineation and disarrangement of both verse and prose in the printed texts of both *The Revenger's Tragedy* and *The Atheist's Tragedy*, the work of early compositors and later editors has been as much under consideration as that of a poet or poets. And the remaining differences discernible may very well be explicable on the grounds of authorial development or the distinctive proprieties of different dramatic contexts.[11] Other kinds of evidence are differently treacherous. Students of the play have been chastened by the fact that two responsible scholars, independently attempting to determine whether the imagery

10 Schoenbaum, "Internal Evidence," p. 122.
11 See Foakes, pp. 130–134; Murray, p. 155.

of the two plays came from one pen, arrived at contradictory conclusions.[12]

From a more general viewpoint we see that fresh critical currents, while they have broadened and deepened our understanding of the play, have only shifted the locus of our uncertainty about its authorship. Some nearly convinced Middletonians, under the spell of T. S. Eliot's still influential view of the play as "an intense and unique and horrible vision of life," a consummate poetic outpouring of adolescent cynicism and loathing of humanity, were inclined to agree that its passionate intensity and moralistic fervor ill sorted with the detached, unmoralistic, apparently objective realism generally associated with Middleton.[13] An important tendency in recent criticism, however, has distinguished more carefully between the author of *The Revenger's Tragedy* and his enmeshed hero, stressed the psychological realism of Vindice's characterization and the ironic controls in the verse, and emphasized the dramatist's investment in and use of traditional resources of moral complaint and satire. The result, for at least one scholar, has been a playwright more within the expected range of Middleton's supposed creative character.[14] But others invested in similar readings are not encouraged to draw this conclusion; and of course the critical sufficiency of the reading itself has not gone unchallenged. Certainly, for many students of the play, it still seems easier to reconcile the differences between it and *The Atheist's Tragedy* than to make sense of the continuity of a career for Middleton which included *The Revenger's Tragedy*.[15]

[12] Marco K. Mincoff, "The Authorship of 'The Revenger's Tragedy,'" *Studia Historico-Philologica Serdicensia*, II (1940), 1–87, and Una Ellis-Fermor, "The Imagery of 'The Revengers Tragedie' and 'The Atheists Tragedie,'" *MLR*, XXX (1935), 289–301; see also Inga-Stina Ekeblad, "An Approach to Tourneur's Imagery," *MLR*, LIV (1959), 489–498.

[13] T. S. Eliot, "Cyril Tourneur," *Selected Essays 1917–1932* (New York, 1952), pp. 165–166; see E. H. C. Oliphant, "Tourneur and 'The Revenger's Tragedy,'" *Times Literary Supplement*, Dec. 18, 1930, p. 1087; Samuel Schoenbaum, "'The Revenger's Tragedy' and Middleton's Moral Outlook," *N & Q*, CXCVI (1951), 9; and Inga-Stina Ekeblad, "On the Authorship of *The Revenger's Tragedy*," *English Studies*, XLI (1960), 239–240.

[14] Murray, pp. 151, 258–259; cf. John Peter, *Complaint and Satire in Early English Literature* (Oxford, 1956), p. 255; Irving Ribner, *Jacobean Tragedy* (New York, 1962), p. 72.

[15] See Harold Jenkins, "Cyril Tourneur," *RES*, XVII (1941), 21–36; L. G. Salingar, "Tourneur and the Tragedy of Revenge," in *The Age of Shakespeare*, ed. Boris Ford (Penguin Books, 1955), pp. 341–342; Robert

Studies based on literary evidence, then, have not produced an overwhelmingly convincing case for either Tourneur or Middleton. Tired with all these, students have resorted to other internal evidence, hopefully less evasive of strict analysis. This has been obtained by bibliographical and linguistic examination of texts. Recently, detailed studies have been made, primarily in the two authors and in this play, of preferred spellings and linguistic forms and the frequency of occurrence of certain pronouns, verbal forms, and colloquial contractions.[16] The classification of some of the evidence as sub-stylistic may be open to some debate, and it may be questioned if there is sufficient evidence of Tourneur's practice in drama to warrant confident application of the method. Yet even so, such evidence as has been considered seems impressively to support the hypothesis that Thomas Middleton must have been responsible for the copy from which *The Revenger's Tragedy* was printed. Of course, even if these forms correlate very strongly with Middleton's practice, sup-posedly that "of no other author," and not with that of Tourneur in his single extant play, the conclusion is only inferentially evidence of *authorship*. The question remains, assuming the data are sufficient and correct, whether we know enough firmly to discredit other hypotheses which might explain them. Furthermore, it must always be remem-bered that these tests are made on texts at least one and perhaps more removes from author's manuscript, so that the inferences supported by their means can only be as adequate as the bibliographical in-ferences upon which they are built. It is perhaps symptomatic that Murray, the student who has most cogently pressed such a case for Middleton, has not only acknowledged this but has felt com-pelled to include a study of this play in his book on Cyril Tourneur.

In sum, the present editor can state with some confidence that he does not know who wrote *The Revenger's Tragedy*. The presence of Tourneur's name on the title page, out of deference to modern publishing tradition and the slender external evidence, and the

Ornstein, *The Moral Vision of Jacobean Tragedy* (Madison, 1960), pp. 105–106; and Ekeblad, "On the Authorship of *The Revenger's Tragedy*."

[16] See Price, pp. 267–269, and the much fuller study in Murray, pp. 158–189, earlier published as "The Authorship of *The Revenger's Tragedy*," *Papers of the Bibliographical Soc. of America*, LVI (1962), 195–218. For the development of the method, see Cyrus Hoy, "The Shares of Fletcher and his Collaborators in the Beaumont and Fletcher Canon (I)," *Studies in Bibliography*, VIII (1956), 129–146.

citation of the scant data about his life and career in the appended chronology, must not be construed to contradict this conclusion.

## SOURCES

No substantial narrative source for the entire action is known, and L. G. Salingar appears justified in supposing that this play, unlike many Elizabethan tragedies, had its genesis not in known story, with its own established logic, but in moral idea and satiric impulse to which useful narrative elements were assimilated within the framework provided by available dramatic conventions.[17] These elements appear to have been drawn from a grab-bag of sources. The rape of Antonio's lady and the subsequent revenge by the company of lords against the nest of dukes probably was suggested by the rape of Lucrece and the banishment of the Tarquins. The episode in which Lussurioso forces his way into the ducal bedchamber apparently can be traced to a story (already used by Sidney) in Heliodorus' *Aethiopian History* (translated by Underdowne, 1587).[18] Interestingly enough, some of the matter seems actually to have been based on incidents in the history of the Medici and the Estensi as retailed in *novelle*. Vindice's procuring of his sister for Lussurioso as well as his management of his revenge against the old Duke himself may have been suggested by the assassination of Allessandro de' Medici after that worthy had asked his nephew Lorenzino to seduce his sister for him. At the rendezvous, Lorenzino produced his murderous villain instead of a paramour. Whoever wrote the play could have been struck by the story in the Queen of Navarre's *Heptaméron* (XII) or in such a translation as that in Painter's *The Palace of Pleasure*.[19] Salingar thinks the maternal part in the seduction may have been hinted by an anecdote about Don Ercole d'Este in Cinthio (and fused with memory of Shakespeare's Gertrude); that further suggestions for the

[17] "*The Revenger's Tragedy*: Some Possible Sources," *MLR*, LX, No. 1 (Jan., 1965), 11–12.

[18] G. K. Hunter, "A Source for *The Revenger's Tragedy*," *RES*, X (1959), 181–182.

[19] See Samuel Schoenbaum, "'The Revenger's Tragedy': A Neglected Source," *N & Q*, CXCV (1950), 338; N. W. Bawcutt, "'The Revenger's Tragedy' and the Medici Family," *N & Q*, CCII (1957), 192–193; and Pierre Legouis, "Réflexions Sur la Recherche des Sources à Propos de la 'Tragédie du Vengeur,'" *Études Anglaises*, XII (1959), 47–55.

Duke may have come from the same novelist's accounts of Niccolò d'Este in the *Hecatommithi*; and that the plot of Ambitioso and Supervacuo for the dukedom may be dependent on the abortive conspiracy in 1506 by two sons of Ercole d'Este against their brothers, noted in Harington's *Ariosto* and reported in Guicciardini's *History of Italy*.[20]

Such "historical" materials have been very freely handled with quite unhistorical ends in view; for the "Italy" of the play's generalized setting of course is not the historic one, but rather the mythic decadent "Italy" of fascinated Elizabethan imagination: the already symbolic "Italy" of perverted sophistication and moral corruption, of atheistic depravity, politic treachery, abandoned sensuality, violence, and vendetta. A common property of the early seventeenth-century English stage, this setting is used, here more brilliantly perhaps than in any other play of the period, for social and economic complaint and embittered moral satire about evils of the contemporary English scene.[21] One measure of the genius which produced *The Revenger's Tragedy* is that the playwright has so realized the quintessence of this Italianate scene that we take its symbolic representation of an evil world to be entirely his own. His deepest indebtednesses are to earlier plays of the native dramatic tradition, in which he is completely at home; and especially to those contemporary ones which showed him how the satiric scene of Italianate corruption might be wedded to the philosophic melodrama of the Kydian-Senecan revenge motive, and to those which suggested how the morality play methods and themes, so accordant with his creative sympathies, might be profoundly used to make the revenge play's mordant ironies more significant and to give allegoric depth to the satire.

There are many evident reminiscences in situation and detail, as well as more subtle influences, of plays in the Kydian convention: *The Spanish Tragedy* itself, *The Jew of Malta*, Chettle's *Hoffman*, and most obviously *Hamlet*. But the most important of such precedent plays for the dramatist plainly are those of Marston, who was the first fully to exploit the sensational possibilities of Italianate revenge and to realize the satiric intensity achievable by placing the malcontent avenger-observer disguised among his enemies in the decadent

[20] "*The Revenger's Tragedy*: Some Possible Sources," pp. 4–11; the relevance of the Don Ercole story in Cinthio's *Novella* VI, iii was earlier noted by Louis Berthé de Besaucèle, *J-B. Giraldi, 1504–1573* (Paris, 1920), p. 208 n.

[21] See Ornstein, pp. 24–26, 116.

Italianate scene. This influence is seen as much in reaction to Marston's work, serving to define and distinguish this author's intent, as in direct indebtedness. His complex and profoundly ironic treatment of Vindice's sadistically "just" murder of the Duke contrasts notably with Marston's morally and artistically incoherent treatment of horrific Italianate vengeance in *Antonio's Revenge*, where the ruthless Senecan revengers, at play's end, are allowed to withdraw from the dirty world to votive contemplation. Even more striking is the reaction to Marston's tragicomedy, *The Malcontent*, much of whose plot this play closely imitates. This is most evident in the depiction of Vindice's deepening cynicism and evil transformation through his revenge. Marston's socially displaced figure (a deposed Duke) plots at the vilely corrupt court of the usurper disguised as a satiric malcontent. He is employed by his enemy, contrives to set his vying foes against each other by exposing their adulteries, is dispatched as pander to his own wife, and in a second disguise is hired to kill his malcontent *persona* (an effective turn also to be found in Middleton's *The Phoenix*). But this "redresser of wrongs," undisillusioned by his bitter satiric vision, regains his untainted identity with his power at the masked revels which conclude the action.[22]

A more congenial influence was exerted by Ben Jonson. His brilliant *Volpone* evidently suggested the general idea of a society of vicious "humours" inevitably drawing to itself an intriguer-satirist who inveigles it to self-destruction through the operation of its own appetites. Clearly, the author admired Jonson's gift for savage farce, for controlled exaggeration and evaluative touch in satiric dialogue, and for sustained moral outlook. Through Jonson's plays too, and especially *Volpone*, came powerful reinforcement of the dramatist's obvious interest in the morality play tradition. As Salingar says, "*The Revenger's Tragedy* is the last, as well as the most brilliant, attempt to present the emotional conflicts of Renaissance society within the framework of moral allegory."[23] The play everywhere betrays its roots in this tradition: in the limited abstract characterizations framed to the symbolic action, in the emblematic treatment of the

[22] See M. C. Bradbrook, *Themes and Conventions of Elizabethan Tragedy* (Cambridge, 1952), p. 165; Salingar, "Tourneur and the Tragedy of Revenge," pp. 341, 344; and Murray, pp. 249–250.
[23] "Tourneur and the Tragedy of Revenge," p. 348. Cf. his important "'The Revenger's Tragedy' and the Morality Tradition," *Scrutiny*, VI (1938), 402–424.

natural world in imagery, in the allegoric action threatening spiritual Chastity, the daughter of Grace. Students have also emphasized the play's patent links with the tradition of medieval moralists: the contrasts of eternity and time and the scornful indignation of *de contemptu mundi* homiletics, the fusion of satirically realistic detail with moral abstraction, the emphatic condemnation of luxury, avarice, and superfluity, and the lashing of judges, lawyers, usurers, and women.[24] The leveling and macabre ironies of the *memento mori* and the Dance of Death (already variously assimilated into English dramatic tradition), wherein Death, the reality of the skull beneath the skin, mocks the worldly blinded by temporal vanities, have been felt to be influential in the play's central symbol, the skull, in the action as deathly dance climaxed in the masque, and in the use of Vindice as moralizing presenter akin to the *Docteur*.[25] Finally, much of the medieval comic spirit plainly survives in the play's self-conscious burlesque, parodic ironies, antic energy, and grotesque exaggeration.[26]

There can be little doubt (though the precise critical significance of the fact may be at issue) that the author's roots went deeply into the pre-Renaissance past. Indeed, it has been convincingly argued that he so identified traditional moral order with the social and economic fabric of the manorial system that abundant evidence of its material disintegration in the Jacobean society about him meant for him the decay and corruption of the order itself.[27] In terms of a mind and sensibility absorbed in such a viewpoint, the extraordinarily charged concreteness of the metaphoric language of the play becomes accountable. And so does its central conflict: between the decadent Italianate court, with ironic propriety emblematic of the larger depraved society of "usury" and prodigal lust of which it is center,

[24] On such medieval tradition in the play, see Peter, pp. 255–287, and Ribner, pp. 72–86.

[25] Samuel Schoenbaum, "*The Revenger's Tragedy*: Jacobean Dance of Death," *Modern Language Quarterly*, XV (1954), 201–207; for the background, see Leonard P. Kurtz, *The Dance of Death and the Macabre Spirit in European Literature* (New York, 1934).

[26] See Willard Farnham, "The Mediaeval Comic Spirit in the English Renaissance," *Joseph Quincy Adams Memorial Studies*, ed. James G. McManaway *et al.* (Washington, 1948), pp. 429–437; A. P. Rossiter, *English Drama from Early Times to the Elizabethans* (London, 1950), pp. 154–155; and Murray, pp. 255–257.

[27] See Salingar, "'The Revenger's Tragedy' and the Morality Tradition."

and the corrupted and liquidated landed values and virtues of the now impoverished and malcontent minor gentry.

## THE PLAY

*The Revenger's Tragedy* is thus a unique fusion of elements from the satiric "humours" comedy, the philosophic revenge melodrama, and the morality and related medieval traditions.[28] Besides study of these, modern criticism has advantageously brought to the play its concern with close reading of poetic texts and its fresh sympathy for the distortive symbolic methods of non-naturalistic drama. The combination has yielded an appreciation of its artistry which largely has replaced late nineteenth-century celebrations of the play as a satanic piece of lurid sensation and macabre horror. The narrowness of its representation of humanity must readily be granted, and so must its lack of those dimensions which Shakespeare's, Jonson's, and Chapman's philosophical and political concerns brought to tragedy. (Indeed, apart from Elizabethan senses of the term, it may be misleading, and a disservice to the play, to think of it as "tragedy.") Yet this drama must now be acknowledged, for dramatic power, for coherence of structure, for astonishing compression and consistency of language, and for superb unity of tone, surpassed in the whole Elizabethan repertory by only the few very greatest plays.

Once this is said, it must be admitted that critics of the play diverge quite as much as students of its authorship, and of course, more often than not, the two inquiries are intertwined. Two large groups may perhaps be abstracted from the multiplicity of critical viewpoints without too great falsification of their actually ranging variety. On the one hand, a band of judgments stresses the artistic objectivity, ironic control, and traditional bases and moral force of the play. Thus, for samples, Murray thinks that the author's careful ironic artistry "argues for his detachment from the 'horror' of the world he portrays and from Vindici's death-motive"; Ribner finds the play in its totality espouses the traditional attitude *de contemptu mundi*; and Peter believes it "is a play where the moral scheme is everything," for "what the second half of the play does is to consolidate and advance the ethical positives that the first half has implied."[29] On the other hand, a spectrum of opinion (often refracting Eliot's light) argues

[28] Ekeblad, "On the Authorship of *The Revenger's Tragedy*," pp. 227 ff.
[29] Murray, p. 254; Ribner, p. 92; Peter, pp. 268, 264.

that the intense narrowness of the play's artificial vision of depravity outweighs the artistic objectivity which makes it possible; in these the drama is found insecurely distanced from the evil it contemplates, or obsessive, or even (in Eliot's phrase) "projected from the author's inner world of nightmare." Thus, Ellis-Fermor thought the author's "definite affirmation of evil stands inflexible and positive"; Fluchère considers he found humanity trapped in a world without spiritual hope; Ornstein believes "cynicism, outrage, loathing, and horror are fused" in the play by the author's "morbid fascination with the erotic" which he has superbly fashioned into a "poetic and dramatic motif"; and Tomlinson argues that "what he actually says constantly modifies traditional attitudes" and that his play triumphs "only precariously over incipient decadence" to which the author himself is drawn.[30]

The play itself may compel us to feel that insights and misconstructions are possibly shared about equally between these camps. Those who find the play obsessive or the playwright insufficiently detached too often have failed to distinguish Vindice's voice (and neuroses) from the author's, to recognize the powerful traditional bases of even the "obsessional" aspects of the play, or to allow the weight its structure gives the important conversion of the fallen Gratiana. Most important, they tend to neglect or underweigh the often implicit, but clearly pervasive, moral referents in the language and action of the play. For their part, those who stress the play's artistic objectivity and traditional morality very frequently tend to flatten the poetry, simplify the ironies, and reduce the traditions involved to common denominators. No doubt the play uses "the very symbols" by which the "philosophy of worldly withdrawal and heavenly contemplation had expressed itself in the Middle Ages."[31] But they are uniquely transformed; and is it merely a flaw in Vindice that prevents him from turning to the other world not merely for reference but (in true *contemptus mundi* fashion) for refuge? To be sure, in the world of the play "Honesty" is always poor, as well as rare; and to get gold is represented as the pollution on entering the

30 Una Ellis-Fermor, *The Jacobean Drama* (London, 1936), p. 153; Henri Fluchère, ed., *La Tragédie du Vengeur* (Paris, 1960), p. 132; Ornstein, pp. 108–110; T. B. Tomlinson, "The Morality of Revenge: Tourneur's Critics," *EIC*, X (1960), 143; cf. the exchange between T. W. Craik and John Peter in *EIC*, VI (1956), 482–486.

31 Ribner, p. 75; cf. Theodore Spencer, *Death and Elizabethan Tragedy* (Cambridge, Mass., 1936), p. 240.

world. Yet it is also malcontent, and by its poverty proves corruptible, used, expended by the wealth that can buy it. To equate such a view with the medieval notion of "holy poverty" is to blanket the bitterness at poverty raging in the literal imagery, and to deny our seeing that social complaint sometimes wrestles with the very moral and religious vision informing it. In the case of Castiza, it is to miss the sourness, the rigidity, the sardonic tone qualifying the confident polarization of moral reality—that is, all that gives the character dimension beyond her allegoric role.

> How hardly shall that maiden be beset
> Whose only fortunes are her constant thoughts,
> That has no other child's-part but her honor,
> That keeps her low and empty in estate.
> Maids and their honors are like poor beginners;
> Were not sin rich, there would be fewer sinners.
> Why had not virtue a revenue? Well,
> I know the cause: 'twould have impoverish'd hell.
>
> (II.i.1–8)

Such critics justly emphasize the true repentance of Gratiana and the importance of what implicitly effects it: the divine grace underscored by the contrasting references to diabolic possession at her temptation. But they rarely indicate the poignant isolation of this spiritual regeneration and the consequent rekindling of familial "kindness" as clearly as Vindice himself wryly does when recalled to the world of his vengeful "business":

> . . . Joy's a subtle elf;
> I think man's happiest when he forgets himself.
>
> (IV.iv.84–85)

More often, they relate it to the supposedly reassuring restoration of ethical standards and moral order at Antonio's accession to the dukedom. Such interpretation is questionable because Antonio is treated with quite as complex an irony at the denouement as any other worldly justicer in the play; his judgments fall within the drama's repetitive pattern of retribution ironically accomplished through injustice. The brothers have earned their condemnation. But his sentencing of them for the vengeance which has temporally benefited him comes immediately after he has appeared to regard

all the murders as heavenly judgments, and pointedly out of fear
for his own vulnerable hide that can now be likened to the old Duke's:

> My good! —Away with 'em. —Such an old man as he!
> You, that would murder him, would murder me!
>
> (V.iii.102–103)

If we are in any doubt, we need only note the blatant parallel which
prepares for the new Duke's reception of Vindice's boasting confession: that between Lussurioso's condemnation of the truthful Gentleman and Antonio's sentencing of Ambitioso and Company's Fourth
accomplice—not for Spurio's murder, of which he is guilty, but for
Duke Lussurioso's, of which he is quite innocent.

It will have been seen that much critical argument turns, not only
upon interpretation of tone and the precise weight to be attributed
to the conventional and traditional, but also on the extent to which
the mind of the author can be inferred from the play. The problem
is complicated by the drama's very conventionality, by the ambiguity of Vindice's role as a special sort of satirist's *persona*,[32] and by
the play's relative lack of direct philosophic or reflective choric
commentary. Yet surely—and this is no doubt partly due to the
limited humanity of its characterizations—few plays, and still
fewer so conventional in basis, leave us with so marked an impression
of the consciousness behind its masks, subtly balancing its complex
apprehensions of the world envisioned through them. And plainly,
much of the tense interest of the play turns upon this inner drama.
Eliot's arresting dogma clearly will no longer quite serve. But more
than one student has felt the play's fascination with the evil it would
ironically behold, and the author's uncertainly poised relation, in the
last analysis, to the traditional values and resources which he pervasively insists are his referents and which indeed deepen the significance, and the pain, of the drama. As Ornstein says, he "has the
scorn and indignation of medieval satirists, not their religious or
moral security."[33] The moralizing couplets center the ranging
great satiric tirades without ever quite reconciling their complexities.
The thunder and comet assure us we are still in the theater of God's

---

[32] See Murray's discussion, pp. 250–252, with reference to O. J. Campbell,
*Comicall Satyre and Shakespeare's Troilus and Cressida* (San Marino, 1938),
pp. 48–57; Peter, pp. 201–206; and Alvin Kernan, *The Cankered Muse:
Satire of the English Renaissance* (New Haven, 1959), p. 227.

[33] P. 117.

judgments, but the eternal's sanctions for action, its grace, and its refuge seem dim amid the temporal world's depravity and decay where its ironic justice manifests itself.

The central theme of the play, realized through its action, emphasized through its pattern of ironic reversals, and everywhere evident in the turns and exchanges of its metaphoric language, is transformation. The society, represented as evilly transformed by gold and usury and appetite, is ruled and adumbrated by a court presented as a procession of Vices, its members reduced to virtual personifications by their lusts. A web of dissembling ambitions and smoldering hatreds, the court, with its abused power, corrupting wealth, and devotion to the "superfluous" outside, epitomizes itself at licentious revels given to gluttonous superfluity and drunken invitation to lust, where night is turned by torchlight to artificial noon, and courtier's masks no longer body forth the virtues of nobility but serve as license for riot, rape, and violence. In the world of perverted values dominated and corrupted by such rule, lordships are sold for whoredoms, land for wardrobes, fruitfields are turned into bastards, and virtue "chang'd/ Into white money." Amid legalistic pleading for sin and oppressive monied power, justice, corrupted by gold and favoritism, is nowhere to be found but in the ironic transformations worked by appetite itself: the profligate reveler melting his usuring father's gold in a whore's kiss. The court, as center of this world, has become a province of the hell that gapes for it; and, driven by their "blood," the sinners of the play, pervasively conscious of their sin as they rush to damnation, prove incapable of any grace but ducal grace, any salvation but worldly salvation.

The appropriate central symbol of the evil transformation wrought by such a death-dealing and death-directed world is the skull of the poisoned chaste and beautiful Gloriana. She stands, of course, for all the betrayed women of the play: Antonio's raped lady, the imagined "country lady" prostituted to the duke in the shape of the masked and costumed skull, and potentially the threatened Castiza herself. But above all, her skull represents the real end to which the society is devoted, the real objective toward which its hectic action moves, and the ultimate reality beneath the masks, the painted cheeks, the dissemblings, disguises, and falsities in a world given to vanity where there is "nothing sure . . . but mortality."

Set apart from the depraved court is the house where Gratiana and Castiza live in neglected virtue and discontented poverty. The play's central action is that in which Vindice travels from Gratiana's house into the world disguised as "a man o'th' time" to seek occasion for his vengeance on the vicious court. Seemingly inverting the convention of the morality play, virtue masks itself as vice.[34] However, given his sardonic knowledge of his world, Vindice's obsession with the corruptibility of what he holds dear soon credibly deepens into reality the role of pander he has assumed. As Fluchère says, he is driven to tempt Castiza out of the very need to prove the existence of the value his vengeance is to affirm.[35] His disillusioning ironic success in tempting his mother deepens his cynicism about the seducibility of virtue so easily "entered." He has staked his "lands in heaven" upon the "blood" of his sister and mother. We trace his loss in the deeper ironies of his murder of the Duke. In carrying out his demonically fitting vengeance, making the poisoner Duke enact his embracing of death through lust, Vindice turns his "lady" from chaste victim into a whore and murderess just as he has turned himself into a pander and murderer. Later disguises confirm his descent into villainy as he and his brother "lose" themselves. In his next masking he plays himself in the role of melancholy indigent scholar, ironically hired to avenge Piato's attempt on his mother and sister's honor. By killing "himself," he grotesquely enacts the meaning of the Duke's murder, stabbing the Duke's body while it is disguised in the Piato costume. For the final triumph of his vengeance he appears in the hated symbol of the decadent court, a masque, in a costume identical with those worn by the murderous step-princes in their parallel ambitious plot against Lussurioso.

The revenge motif which figures in almost every part of the plot[36]— in both the Duchess' and Spurio's motives for incestuous adultery, in Ambitioso's and Supervacuo's rivalry, hatred of Spurio, and attempts on Lussurioso, and in Lussurioso's own fury at Piato—also inevitably works parodically to place Vindice and Hippolito's vengeance in ironic perspective. Ultimately, their "minute" of vengeance becomes no different from the "bewitching minute" of sensual pleasure, the "vicious minute" of virtue's ravishment, or the momentary realization

---

[34] See Salingar, "'The Revenger's Tragedy' and the Morality Tradition," pp. 409–411, and Murray, p. 192.

[35] P. 65.

[36] See, on this iteration of the motive, Henry Hitch Adams, "Cyril Tourneur on Revenge," *Journal of English and Germanic Philology*, XLVIII (1949), 72–87.

of the absurd hope of the ambitious ("duke in a minute"!): all become the moment in which "honest salvation is betray'd to sin."

The play's structure is an elaborate complex of ironic reversals of intent and expectation,[37] and these enforce both the theme of transformation and the emphatic contrast between the blindered mortal plotting and the judgmental providence of "that eternal eye/ That sees through flesh and all." By parallelism, iteration, and scenic juxtaposition many of these reversals are made to comment on the central revengers' tragedy. This is perhaps seen most easily in the paired ironic frustrations of Lussurioso's attempt to save his father's honor while Spurio tries to trap him at his lust for Castiza; but the course of Ambitioso and Supervacuo best confirms the point. The ironic success of their feigned pleading for Lussurioso and the disastrous result of their scheme to save their brother underscore Piato's success as "sin's attorney," and the transformed meaning of Vindice's vengeance. Later, Vindice's exultation over the tortured, dead Duke is dramatically paired by crosscut with their vying for honors for Lussurioso's death, supposedly accomplished by the intriguing that actually has cost the neck of the brother they hoped to save. A brief scene in which they resolve to put a stop to their mother's incestuous adultery is juxtaposed with Vindice and Hippolito's enforced conversion of their bawd-turned mother; this prepares for the final ironic parallel of the two sets of murderous masquers—one motivated by ambition, the other by vengeance—aiming at the same victims. The climax of the pattern of ironic reversals comes with the compounded ironies, prepared for by it, at Vindice's self-disclosure of his "well-manag'd" crimes.

Few Elizabethan dramatic actions move with this play's closely conducted rapidity of pace, and fewer have its hypnotic fascination once we give ourselves to them. If we allow its poetry to compel our acceptance of the unrealistic action through which its significance and its conviction burn, the drama's effect is inescapably overpowering. And this is not merely a matter (as so often in the frequently disjointed Elizabethan drama) of a few striking scenes. It is perhaps, above all, to say that its poetry is much of the time very great dramatic poetry, histrionically erupting from the fierce vision producing the action. The opening monologue, the temptation scenes, the stunning apostrophes to night, and above all, the incomparable "silkworm"

[37] See Bradbrook, pp. 165 ff.; also Peter Lisca, "*The Revenger's Tragedy:* A Study in Irony," *Philological Quarterly*, XXXVIII (1959), 242–251.

speech addressed to the costumed skull are deservedly prized, not as isolated verbal "beauties of Tourneur," but because the metaphoric terms of the play's sense of reality here achieve their most tersely compelling expression.

> Does the silkworm expend her yellow labors
> For thee? for thee does she undo herself?
> Are lordships sold to maintain ladyships
> For the poor benefit of a bewitching minute?
> Why does yon fellow falsify highways,
> And put his life between the judge's lips,
> To refine such a thing, keeps horse and men
> To beat their valors for her?
> Surely we're all mad people, and they
> Whom we think are, are not: we mistake those;
> 'Tis we are mad in sense, they but in clothes.
>
> (III.v.71–81)

Such awesome concentration of almost palpable meaning would seem inevitably to have come from profoundly and immediately jarred, if richly traditional, simplicities of vision. Perhaps that is why there is nothing, even in the very much greater, differently complex, and farther ranging Shakespeare, quite like this, so narrowly focused in imaginative power, so acrid in its subtlety.

## THE TEXT

The publication dated 1607 in which *The Revenger's Tragedy* was first issued is a quarto collating A–I4: A1r title page, A1v blank, A2r to I4v text. A variant of this edition dated 1608, made up of the same sheets (and, in the past, sometimes supposed a separate edition or another issue with a fresh title page), is bibliographically distinguishable only by the change of the last digit and an insignificant shift of the lower type on A1r. The other press variants appear variously in examplars of the quarto with the differently dated title pages.

The stage directions suggest that the quarto was printed from a manuscript neither fully prepared for a reading public (as that for *The Atheist's Tragedy* evidently was), nor worked over for use in the theater. Many requisite directions are missing or defective; anticipatory ones calling for the readying of properties and so forth are lacking; and the long, descriptive directions at V.iii.0.1–3 and 48.1–5 are not of the variety normally encountered in a text based on a theatrical promptbook. From this evidence, from the general soundness of the text, and from the presence of spellings unlikely to have been compositorial in origin, we may judge that the copy of the quarto must not have been at too distant a remove, if any, from the author's manuscript. Faithfulness to the copy in the printing is indicated by the difficulty which the bibliographer encounters in attempting to distinguish between (or, perhaps, among) compositors.[38]

Fortunately, then, this text in which the play is preserved to us is, in general, substantively good. The quarto's punctuation and lineation, however, are much less reliable than its language. The pointing is not in most respects notably worse than that in comparable publications; but the text is peppered with question marks, the printers either having spilled these among the other marks or run out of periods. The lineation problem is more complex and also more serious, as it affects not merely our grasp of the playwright's poetic art but also, since prosodic arguments for authorship have been proffered, our opinions as to his identity. Such arguments are meaningless without reference to the adequacy in this respect of the edition used.

There can be little question that many passages need rearrangement. The compositors evidently were confronted by a manuscript in which prose and verse were mixed and not always clearly distinguished: in which there were abrupt prose-verse transitions, passages of prose within verse speeches, and, occasionally, prose rhythms within the verse itself. In addition, we have evidence for a tendency to build up to pentameters by shorter verse lines and to precede or interrupt blank verse patterns with short or hypermetrical lines. In dealing with these complexities, the compositors display a tendency to run verse into prose; at points also they anticipate the predilection of some later editors by making verse out of prose; and they frequently obscure shared lines and place extra half-lines of verse on the same line with the properly preceding or following full pentameter.

Editors disagree substantially as to the correct arrangement, and the present one has space only to offer, with some diffidence, the

38 See Price, pp. 272–273, and for his conclusion that the manuscript used by the printers was a fair copy in Middleton's hand, pp. 263 ff.

results of his own study of the problem. The textual notes of the present edition, however, do record each instance where the copy-text's verse has been turned into prose or its prose into verse.

The present text is freshly based on the 1607–1608 quarto, the only seventeenth-century edition. In order to detect alterations of the text while the sheets were being printed, the editor collated the nine exemplars of the quarto known by him to be located in the United States: those bearing the "1607" title page in the Boston Public, Folger, Huntington, Clark, Yale, Houghton, and Chapin Libraries, and those with the "1608" title page in the Folger and Huntington. Such proofing of the sheets as was done evidently was not performed by the author of the play. Twenty-nine corrections were observed on pages of signatures A, D, E, F, and G and on several pages of signature H, on the outer forme of which two stages of alteration (here designated states 2 and 3) can be distinguished. These press variants, wherever they affect substantive readings, are recorded in the textual notes.

In keeping with the principles governing this series, contracted forms of character's names in speech prefixes have been silently emended and the names themselves regularized, *Vindice* (the quarto's most frequent form of the hero's name) thus replacing its various spellings. For clarity's sake, I have also substituted *Gratiana* and *Youngest Son* for the *Mother* and *Iunior* generally found in the copy-text. Misprints, if unquestionably such, have been silently emended. Since punctuation has been brought into accord with modern usage, noting of departures from the copy-text in this respect has been limited to those few occasions where alteration of the pointing quite changes the sense. A similar practice has been adopted with regard to the spelling, which has been modernized, original orthography being retained only where essential to meter, sense, or wordplay. The textual notes do not record the quarto's early seventeenth-century orthographic forms (such as *loose* for "lose," *sild* for "seld") where these involve no ambiguity; but cases which may mask substantive variation have been noted.

LAWRENCE J. ROSS

Washington University, St. Louis

# THE REVENGER'S TRAGEDY

# [DRAMATIS PERSONAE

THE DUKE
LUSSURIOSO, *the Duke's son*
SPURIO, *his bastard son*
AMBITIOSO, *the Duchess' eldest son*
SUPERVACUO, *the Duchess' second son*                                      5
THE YOUNGEST SON *of the Duchess*
VINDICE, *the revenger, sometimes disguised as* PIATO ⎫
HIPPOLITO, *his brother, also called* CARLO ⎬ *sons of Gratiana*
ANTONIO, *an old lord*                                                     ⎭
PIERO, *a lord*                                                            10
DONDOLO, *servant of Castiza*
JUDGES, NOBLES, GENTLEMEN, OFFICERS, KEEPER, GUARDS, *and*
    SERVANTS, *two named* NENCIO *and* SORDIDO

THE DUCHESS
CASTIZA, *sister of Vindice and Hippolito*                                 15
GRATIANA, *a widow, their mother*

Scene: *A duchy of Italy*]

*Dramatis Personae*] *not in* Q.

---

*Dramatis Personae*] The descriptive Italianate names emphasize the symbolic bias in characterization.
  2. *Lussurioso*] "leacherous, luxurious, lustfull" (Florio).
  3. *Spurio*] "a whores sonne whose father is not know[n], a bastard, one baseborne. vsed also for a counterfeit" (Florio).
  4. *Ambitioso*] "ambitious, very desirous of honour" (Florio).
  5. *Supervacuo*] "too much, superfluous, ouermuch vaine, not necessarie, vnprofitable, to no vse" (Florio).
  7. *Vindice*] "a reuenger of wrongs. a redresser of things, and abuses . . ." (Florio).
  7. *Piato*] "a plea, a suit in law, a controuersie, a processe, a pleading. Also [translating modern Italian *piatto*] flat, squat, cowred downe, hidden . . ." (Florio).
  11. *Dondolo*] "a gull, a foole, a thing to make sport" (Florio); here perhaps also with reference to Italian *dondolone*, idler. A name possibly drawn from Marston's *Parasitaster, or The Fawn* (Nicoll).
  13. *Nencio*] "a foole, an idiot, a naturall, a doult, a gull" (Florio); but here, apparently, also with punning reference to *nuntius*.
  13. *Sordido*] "absurd, filthy, corrupt, vncleane, beastly . . ." (Florio).
  15. *Castiza*] chastity; from *casta*, chaste.
  16. *Gratiana*] grace (for a time, ironically appropriate); probably from *gratia*, "a grace, a pardon" (Florio).

# The Revenger's Tragedy

**[I.i]**

*Enter* Vindice [*with a skull in his hand*]. *The Duke; Duchess; Lussurioso, his son; Spurio, the bastard; with a train, pass over the stage with torchlight.*

VINDICE.

>Duke! royal lecher! Go, gray-hair'd adultery,
>And thou his son, as impious steep'd as he,
>And thou his bastard true-begot in evil,
>And thou his duchess that will do with devil:
>Four exc'lent characters. —O, that marrowless age          5
>Should stuff the hollow bones with damn'd desires,
>And 'stead of heat kindle infernal fires
>Within the spendthrift veins of a dry duke,
>A parch'd and juiceless luxur. O God! one

0.1.] *Q heads ACT. I. SCÆ. I., similarly divides at II and IV, specifies Act only at III. Neither act division at*    V, *nor scene division elsewhere is indicated.*
0.2. *his*] *her Q.*
6. Should] *Dodsley;* Would *Q.*

---

1. *royal*] sarcastic: with magnificence befitting a sovereign, splendid.
1. *gray-hair'd adultery*] the Duke viewed as the symbolic personification of his sin.
4. *do*] perform the sexual act; see Partridge, p. 103.
5. *exc'lent*] egregious.
5. *characters*] in the Jacobean literary sense, as L. G. Salingar notes (p. 342); rhetorically heightened exemplary portraits of types or abstracted qualities of good or evil.
7–11. *heat . . . heir*] based, like other lines associating blood and erotic passion (cf. II.ii.92), on Renaissance physiology. In its given amount of blood reside heat and moisture, the essential qualities of the living body. Youth is "sanguine"; "aging is a process of cooling and drying." Since blood is the material cause of semen, and "a great deal . . . goes into the generation of a small amount," incontinence is injurious prodigality. See Lawrence Babb, "The Physiological Concept of Love in the Elizabethan and Early Stuart Drama," *PMLA*, LVI (1941), 1020–1035.
9. *luxur*] lecher.

That has scarce blood enough to live upon,       10
And he to riot it like a son and heir?
O the thought of that
Turns my abused heartstrings into fret.—
[*Addressing the skull.*] Thou sallow picture of my poisoned
    love,
My studies' ornament, thou shell of death,       15
Once the bright face of my betrothed lady,
When life and beauty naturally fill'd out
These ragged imperfections,
When two heaven-pointed diamonds were set
In those unsightly rings—then 'twas a face       20
So far beyond the artificial shine
Of any woman's bought complexion
That the uprightest man (if such there be,
That sin but seven times a day) broke custom
And made up eight with looking after her:       25
O she was able to ha' made a usurer's son
Melt all his patrimony in a kiss,
And what his father fifty yeares told
To have consum'd, and yet his suit been cold.
But O accursed palace!       30
Thee, when thou wert apparell'd in thy flesh,
The old duke poison'd,
Because thy purer part would not consent
Unto his palsy-lust; for old men lustful
Do show like young men angry, eager-violent,       35
Outbid like their limited performances.
O 'ware an old man hot and vicious.

---

13. *Turns . . . fret*] *OED* cites to illustrate *fret* in the sense of "agitation of mind"; but this neglects the implied musical figure based on the commonplace image of man as, physically and spiritually, a stringed instrument. See Gretchen L. Finney, "A World of Instruments," *ELH*, XX (1953) and, e.g., Chapman, *Monsieur D'Olive*: "The string sounds euer well that rubs not too much ath frets."

15. *studies*'] double in meaning when spoken. As a *memento mori* and symbol of the vanity of life, the skull of course was a pictorial commonplace.

15. *shell of death*] a typical ambiguity; cf. I.i.50.

28. *yeares*] disyllabic. The poet is fond of such survivals of the older voiced inflectional endings.

28. *told*] counted.     37. *vicious*] trisyllabic.

"Age as in gold, in lust is covetous."—
Vengeance, thou murder's quit-rent, and whereby
Thou show'st thyself tenant to Tragedy,                    40
O keep thy day, hour, minute, I beseech,
For those thou hast determin'd. Hum! who e'er knew
Murder unpaid? faith, give Revenge her due,
Sh'as kept touch hitherto. —Be merry, merry;
Advance thee, O thou terror to fat folks,                    45
To have their costly three-pil'd flesh worn off
As bare as this—for banquets, ease, and laughter
Can make great men, as greatness goes by clay,
But wise men little are more great than they!

*Enter his brother* Hippolito.

HIPPOLITO.
Still sighing o'er death's vizard?
VINDICE.                              Brother, welcome!                    50
What comfort bring'st thou? how go things at court?
HIPPOLITO.
In silk and silver, brother: never braver.
VINDICE.
Pooh,
Thou play'st upon my meaning. Prithee say,
Has that bald madam, Opportunity,                    55
Yet thought upon's? speak, are we happy yet?

40 show'st]   *Dodsley*   (shew'st);   46. off] *Dodsley;* of *Q*.
shoust *Q*.                                   49.1. *his*] *Dodsley; her Q*.

---

38. Sententious phrases are often set off with quotation marks in seventeenth-century editions.

39. *quit-rent*] literally, "a rent paid by a free-holder or copy-holder in lieu of services which might be required of him" (*OED*); but the idea of substitute payment appears de-emphasized in favor of the play on *quit* in the sense of "repayment for an injury"; Vengeance shows itself *tenant to Tragedy* by paying a kind of *quit-rent*: it proves the requital of murder.

46. *three-pil'd*] figuratively applying the name for the richest kind of velvet.

50. *vizard*] (1) mask; (2) "a face or countenance suggestive of a mask" (*OED*).

55. *bald madam*] Opportunity (Occasion) was personified in the Renaissance as a bald, nude, winged female with a single forelock which had to be seized in time; cf. I.i.99–100. See Panofsky, pp. 71–72, for the pertinence of the motif to the theme of time and the moment.

Thy wrongs and mine are for one scabbard fit.

HIPPOLITO.

It may prove happiness.

VINDICE.                    What is't may prove?

Give me to taste.

HIPPOLITO.          Give me your hearing then.

You know my place at court.

VINDICE.                         Ay, the duke's chamber.          60

But 'tis a marvel thou'rt not turn'd out yet!

HIPPOLITO.

Faith, I have been shov'd at, but 'twas still my hap

To hold by th' duchess' skirt: you guess at that;

Whom such a coat keeps up can ne'er fall flat.

But to the purpose.                                         65

Last evening, predecessor unto this,

The duke's son warily inquir'd for me,

Whose pleasure I attended. He began

By policy to open and unhusk me

About the time and common rumor;                            70

But I had so much wit to keep my thoughts

Up in their built houses, yet afforded him

An idle satisfaction without danger.

But the whole aim and scope of his intent

Ended in this: conjuring me in private,                     75

To seek some strange-digested fellow forth

Of ill-contented nature, either disgrac'd

In former times, or by new grooms displac'd

Since his stepmother's nuptials; such a blood,

A man that were for evil only good:                         80

To give you the true word, some base-coin'd pander.

VINDICE.

I reach you; for I know his heat is such,

Were there as many concubines as ladies,

He would not be contain'd; he must fly out.

I wonder how ill-featur'd, vild-proportion'd               85

62. shov'd] *Dodsley;* shooud *Q.*          78. displac'd] *Dodsley;* displacst *Q.*
77. disgrac'd] *Dodsley;* disgracst *Q.*

---

64. *coat*] skirt.

76. *strange-digested*] singularly "disposed, conditioned" (*OED*).

81. *base-coin'd*] basely conceived.          85. *vild-*] vilely.

That one should be, if she were made for woman,
Whom at the insurrection of his lust
He would refuse for once; heart, I think none,
Next to a skull, though more unsound than one.
Each face he meets he strongly dotes upon.          90

HIPPOLITO.

Brother, y'ave truly spoke him.
He knows not you, but I'll swear you know him.

VINDICE.

And therefore I'll put on that knave for once,
And be a right man then, a man o'th' time;
For to be honest is not to be i'th' world.          95
Brother, I'll be that strange-composed fellow.

HIPPOLITO.

And I'll prefer you, brother.

VINDICE.                    Go to, then.
The small'st advantage fattens wronged men.
It may point out Occasion; if I meet her,
I'll hold her by the foretop fast enough;          100
Or like the French mole heave up hair and all.
I have a habit that will fit it quaintly.

[*Enter* Gratiana *and* Castiza.]

Here comes our mother.

HIPPOLITO.               And sister.

VINDICE.                    We must coin.

| | |
|---|---|
| 97. to] *Dodsley;* too *Q*. | occasion, *Q*. |
| 98–99. men./ . . . out  Occasion;] | 101. mole] *Reed; Moale Q*. |
| *Dodsley*  (men:);  men/ . . . out, | 103. coin] *Dodsley;* quoyne *Q*. |

---

93. *put on*] "to take upon oneself, adopt, assume (a character or quality, real or feigned)" (*OED*).

94. *right*] "justly entitled to the name, having the true character of" (*OED*); with sarcastic undermeaning, "upright."

97. *prefer you*] promote your advancement.

99–100. *Occasion . . . enough*] cf. I.i.55, note.

101. *French mole*] evidently a translation of French *taulpier*, "an impostume, or soft swelling in the head, wherein it makes a hole somewhat like that which a mole roots in the ground" (Cotgrave).

102. *habit*] costume.

102. *quaintly*] (1) "ingeniously, so as to accomplish some act or attain some end"; (2) finely, elegantly (*OED*).

103. *coin*] counterfeit.

Women are apt, you know, to take false money;
But I dare stake my soul for these two creatures;                105
Only excuse excepted, that they'll swallow,
Because their sex is easy in belief.

GRATIANA.
What news from court, son Carlo?

HIPPOLITO.                              Faith, mother,
'Tis whisper'd there the duchess' youngest son
Has play'd a rape on Lord Antonio's wife.                        110

GRATIANA.
On that religious lady!

CASTIZA.
Royal blood! monster, he deserves to die,
If Italy had no more hopes but he.

VINDICE.
Sister, y'ave sentenc'd most direct, and true;
The law's a woman, and would she were you.—                     115
Mother, I must take leave of you.

GRATIANA.
Leave for what?

VINDICE.                I intend speedy travail.

HIPPOLITO.
That he does, madam.

GRATIANA.                        Speedy indeed!

VINDICE.
For since my worthy father's funeral,
My life's unnaturally to me, e'en compell'd,                     120
As if I liv'd now when I should be dead.

GRATIANA.
Indeed, he was a worthy gentleman,
Had his estate been fellow to his mind.

108. court] *Dodsley;* Cour *Q.*          112. Royal blood! monster,] *Dods-*
*ley;* Royall bloud:monster *Q.*

---

105–107. *But . . . belief*] Though not seducible in moral matters, they
will readily swallow our excuse because, as women, they are credulous by
nature.

112. *Royal blood*] This sarcastic ejaculation about the blood royal assumes
the meanings noted above at ll. 1 and 7.

113. *If*] even if.

117. *travail*] travel, with pun on *travail*, "labor": Vindice means to make
quick work of his vengeance.

VINDICE.
> The duke did much deject him.

GRATIANA.                              Much!

VINDICE.                                        Too much.
> And through disgrace oft smother'd in his spirit,        125
> When it would mount; surely I think he died
> Of discontent, the nobleman's consumption.

GRATIANA.
> Most sure he did.

VINDICE.                    Did he? 'lack. You know all;
> You were his midnight secretary.

GRATIANA.                              No.
> He was too wise to trust me with his thoughts.          130

VINDICE.
> I'faith then, father, thou wast wise indeed;
> "Wives are but made to go to bed and feed."
> Come mother, sister. —You'll bring me onward, brother?

HIPPOLITO.
> I will.

VINDICE [aside]. I'll quickly turn into another.          *Exeunt.*


[I.ii]

*Enter the old* Duke; Lussurioso, *his son;* the Duchess; [Spurio,] *the*
*bastard;* the Duchess' *two sons,* Ambitioso *and* Supervacuo; *the third,*
*her* Youngest [Son], *brought out with Officers for the rape.* Two Judges.

DUKE.
> Duchess, it is your youngest son, we're sorry;
> His violent act has e'en drawn blood of honor
> And stain'd our honors;
> Thrown ink upon the forehead of our state
> Which envious spirits will dip their pens into          5
> After our death, and blot us in our tombs.

124. Too] *Dodsley;* To *Q.*

---

4. *Thrown . . . forehead*] initiates an important motif. Apart from references to cuckoldry, *forehead* is "used for the countenance as capable of
expressing shame" in two opposed senses: (1) capable of blushing, sense of
shame; (2) unblushing impudence (*OED*). See, specifically regarding the
writing the shame of unchastity upon the forehead, Rev. 17:5 and *Othello*
IV.ii.71-72.
5. *envious*] malicious.

For that which would seem treason in our lives
Is laughter when we're dead. Who dares now whisper
That dares not then speak out, and e'en proclaim
With loud words and broad pens our closest shame. 10

FIRST JUDGE.

Your grace hath spoke like to your silver years,
Full of confirmed gravity; for what is it to have
A flattering false insculption on a tomb,
And in men's hearts reproach? The bowel'd corpse
May be cer'd in, but with free tongue I speak, 15
"The faults of great men through their cerecloths break."

DUKE.

They do, we're sorry for't; it is our fate
To live in fear and die to live in hate.
I leave him to your sentence; doom him, lords—
The fact is great—whilst I sit by and sigh. 20

DUCHESS [kneeling].

My gracious lord, I pray be merciful,
Although his trespass far exceed his years.
Think him to be your own as I am yours;
Call him not son-in-law: the law I fear
Will fall too soon upon his name and him. 25
Temper his fault with pity!

LUSSURIOSO.                        Good my lord,
Then 'twill not taste so bitter and unpleasant
Upon the judges' palate; for offences
Gilt o'er with mercy show like fairest women,
Good only for their beauties, which wash'd off, 30
No sin is uglier.

AMBITIOSO.                I beseech your grace,

11.S.P.] *Iud. Q*.                    30. their] *Dodsley;* therr *Q*.
16. cerecloths] *Reed* (serecloths);    30. off] *Dodsley;* of *Q*.
searce clothes *Q*.

---

10. *broad pens*] writings (1) plainspoken, (2) gross, (3) widely diffused
(*OED*).
13. *insculption*] carved inscription.
14. *bowel'd*] disemboweled, in being prepared for burial.
15. *cer'd in*] embalmed and wrapped in *cerecloths* (l. 16), i.e., waxed
sheets.
20. *fact*] crime.

Be soft and mild; let not relentless law
Look with an iron forehead on our brother.
SPURIO [*aside*].
    He yields small comfort yet, hope he shall die;
    And if a bastard's wish might stand in force,      35
    Would all the court were turn'd into a corse.
DUCHESS.
    No pity yet? Must I rise fruitless then?
    A wonder in a woman! Are my knees
    Of such low metal, that without respect—
FIRST JUDGE.
    Let the offender stand forth:      40
    'Tis the duke's pleasure that impartial doom
    Shall take fast hold of his unclean attempt.
    A rape! why, 'tis the very core of lust,
    Double adultery.
YOUNGEST SON.      So, sir.
SECOND JUDGE.      And which was worse,
    Committed on the Lord Antonio's wife,      45
    That general honest lady. Confess, my lord,
    What mov'd you to't?
YOUNGEST SON.      Why, flesh and blood, my lord.
    What should move men unto a woman else?
LUSSURIOSO.
    O do not jest thy doom; trust not an axe
    Or sword too far: the law is a wise serpent      50
    And quickly can beguile thee of thy life.
    Though marriage only has made thee my brother,
    I love thee so far: play not with thy death.
YOUNGEST SON.
    I thank you, troth; good admonitions, faith,
    If I'd the grace now to make use of them.      55
FIRST JUDGE.
    That lady's name has spread such a fair wing
    Over all Italy, that if our tongues

42. fast] *Dodsley;* first *Q*.

---

36. *corse*] corpse.
42. *unclean*] unchaste.
46. *general honest*] completely chaste and upright.

Were sparing toward the fact, judgment itself
Would be condemned and suffer in men's thoughts.

YOUNGEST SON.

Well then, 'tis done, and it would please me well    60
Were it to do again: sure she's a goddess,
For I'd no power to see her, and to live.
It falls out true in this, for I must die;
Her beauty was ordain'd to be my scaffold.
And yet, methinks, I might be easier cess'd:    65
My fault being sport, let me but die in jest.

FIRST JUDGE.

This be the sentence—

DUCHESS.

O keep't upon your tongue, let it not slip;
Death too soon steals out of a lawyer's lip.
Be not so cruel-wise!

FIRST JUDGE.    Your grace must pardon us;  70
'Tis but the justice of the law.

DUCHESS.    The law
Is grown more subtle than a woman should be.

SPURIO [aside].

Now, now he dies; rid 'em away.

DUCHESS [aside].

O what it is to have an old-cool duke,
To be as slack in tongue as in performance.    75

FIRST JUDGE.

Confirm'd, this be the doom irrevocable.

DUCHESS.

O!

FIRST JUDGE. Tomorrow early—

DUCHESS.    Pray be abed, my lord.

FIRST JUDGE.

Your grace much wrongs yourself.

AMBITIOSO.    No, 'tis that tongue;

65. methinks] *Dodsley;* my thinks  65. cess'd] ceast *Q.*
*Q.*

---

65. *cess'd*] aphetic form of "assessed" (*OED*), with probable secondary
sense, "stopped, caused to cease" (Nicoll).
66. *sport*] (1) amorous dalliance; (2) a pleasant pastime, a mere game.

Your too much right does do us too much wrong.

FIRST JUDGE.
    Let that offender—
DUCHESS.                        Live, and be in health.                    80
FIRST JUDGE.
    —Be on a scaffold—
DUKE.                        Hold, hold, my lord!
SPURIO [aside].                                        Pox on't,
    What makes my dad speak now?
DUKE.
    We will defer the judgment till next sitting;
    In the meantime, let him be kept close prisoner.—
    Guard, bear him hence.
AMBITIOSO [to Youngest Son]. Brother, this makes for thee;        85
    Fear not, we'll have a trick to set thee free.
YOUNGEST SON [apart].
    Brother, I will expect it from you both;
    And in that hope I rest.
SUPERVACUO.                        Farewell, be merry.
                                Exit [Youngest Son] with a guard.
SPURIO [aside].
    Delay'd, deferr'd! Nay then, if judgment have
    Cold blood, flattery and bribes will kill it.                    90
DUKE.
    About it, then, my lords, with your best powers;
    More serious business calls upon our hours.
                                Exeunt; manet Duchess.
DUCHESS.
    Was't ever known step-duchess was so mild
    And calm as I? Some now would plot his death
    With easy doctors, those loose-living men,                    95
    And make his wither'd grace fall to his grave,
    And keep church better.

81. Pox] Dodsley; Pax Q.            87–88.] Reed; prose in Q.

---

85. makes for thee] operates in your favor (OED).
92.1. manet Duchess] the Duchess remains.
    96. wither'd grace] spiritual as well as literal (a duke being referred to as
"his grace").
    97. keep church better] The wit assumes a duke's privileged burial within
the church itself.

Some second wife would do this, and dispatch
Her double-loath'd lord at meat, and sleep.
Indeed 'tis true an old man's twice a child;                    100
Mine cannot speak; one of his single words
Would quite have freed my youngest dearest son
From death or durance, and have made him walk
With a bold foot upon the thorny law,
Whose prickles should bow under him. But 'tis not,              105
And therefore wedlock faith shall be forgot.
I'll kill him in his forehead; hate, there feed;
That wound is deepest though it never bleed.

[*Enter* Spurio.]

And here comes he whom my heart points unto,
His bastard son, but my love's true-begot;                      110
Many a wealthy letter have I sent him,
Swell'd up with jewels, and the timorous man
Is yet but coldly kind.
That jewel's mine that quivers in his ear,
Mocking his master's chillness and vain fear.                   115
H'as spied me now.
SPURIO.                    Madam, your grace so private?
My duty on your hand.
DUCHESS.
Upon my hand, sir. Troth, I think you'd fear
To kiss my hand too if my lip stood there.
SPURIO.
Witness I would not, madam.            [*He kisses her.*]
DUCHESS.                    'Tis a wonder,                       120
For ceremony has made many fools.
It is as easy way unto a duchess
As to a hatted dame, if her love answer;
But that by timorous honors, pale respects,
Idle degrees of fear, men make their ways                       125
Hard of themselves. What have you thought of me?

---

107. *forehead*] reference to the cuckold's horns.
123. *hatted dame*] a woman of the lower orders; noble ladies did not wear
"hats."

SPURIO.

    Madame, I ever think of you in duty,

    Regard, and—

DUCHESS.         Pooh! upon my love, I mean.

SPURIO.

    I would 'twere love, but 'tas a fouler name

    Than lust; you are my father's wife;         130

    Your grace may guess now what I could call it.

DUCHESS.

    Why, th'art his son but falsely;

    'Tis a hard question whether he begot thee.

SPURIO.

    I'faith, 'tis true too; I'm an uncertain man

    Of more uncertain woman. May be his groom    135

    O'th' stable begot me; you know I know not.

    He could ride a horse well: a shrewd suspicion, marry!

    He was wondrous tall; he had his length, i'faith,

    For peeping over half-shut holyday windows:

    Men would desire him light. When he was afoot    140

    He made a goodly show under a pent-house;

    And when he rid, his hat would check the signs,

    And clatter barbers' basins.

DUCHESS.         Nay, set you a-horseback once,

    You'll ne'er light off.

SPURIO.         Indeed, I am a beggar.

DUCHESS.

    That's more the sign thou'rt great. —But to our love.    145

    Let it stand firm, both in thought and mind,

---

129. 'tas] 'tus *Q*.            145. thou'rt] *Dodsley;* thou'art *Q*.

135–139.] *Hazlitt; prose in Q*.

---

    137. *ride a horse*] with obscene secondary sense.

    140. *light*] alight. They wanted him dismounted because on horseback he was so tall that he could peep at their private use of holydays even though the bottom halves of windows were shuttered.

    141. *pent-house*] the sloping eaves of a roof.

    142. *check*] collide with.

    143. *barbers' basins*] used as barbers' signs.

    143–144. *set . . . beggar*] the proverb (Tilley, B 238) "Set a beggar on horseback and he will ride a gallop (will never alight)" applied sexually.

That the duke was thy father, as no doubt then
He bid fair for't: thy injury is the more;
For had he cut thee a right diamond,
Thou hadst been next set in the dukedom's ring,                    150
When his worn self, like age's easy slave,
Had dropp'd out of the collet into th' grave.
What wrong can equal this? Canst thou be tame
And think upon't?

SPURIO.                            No, mad and think upon't.

DUCHESS.

Who would not be reveng'd of such a father,                         155
E'en in the worst way? I would thank that sin
That could most injury him, and be in league with it.
O what a grief 'tis, that a man should live
But once i'th' world, and then to live a bastard,
The curse o'the womb, the thief of nature,                         160
Begot against the seventh commandement,
Half damn'd in the conception by the justice
Of that unbribed everlasting law.

SPURIO.

O, I'd a hot-back'd devil to my father.

DUCHESS.

Would not this mad e'en patience, make blood rough?                165
Who but an eunuch would not sin? his bed,
By one false minute disinherited.

SPURIO.

Ay, there's the vengeance that my birth was wrapp'd in!
I'll be reveng'd for all. Now, hate, begin;
I'll call foul incest but a venial sin.                            170

DUCHESS.

Cold still: in vain then must a duchess woo?

SPURIO.

Madam, I blush to say what I will do.

DUCHESS.

Thence flew sweet comfort. Earnest, and farewell.

                                        [*She kisses him.*]

---

152. *collet*] "that part of a ring in which the stone is set" (Johnson).
157. *injury*] injure.
161. *commandement*] The "e" is sounded.    165. *rough*] violent.
173. *Earnest*] The kiss is a pledge of the future full reward.

SPURIO.

O, one incestuous kiss picks open hell.

DUCHESS.

Faith, now, old duke, my vengeance shall reach high;        175
I'll arm thy brow with woman's heraldry.        *Exit* [Duchess].

SPURIO.

Duke, thou didst do me wrong, and by thy act
Adultery is my nature.
Faith, if the truth were known, I was begot
After some gluttonous dinner; some stirring dish        180
Was my first father: when deep healths went round,
And ladies' cheeks were painted red with wine,
Their tongues, as short and nimble as their heels,
Uttering words sweet and thick; and when they rose,
Were merrily dispos'd to fall again.        185
In such a whisp'ring and withdrawing hour,
When base male-bawds kept sentinel at stair-head,
Was I stol'n softly. O, damnation met!
The sin of feasts, drunken adultery:
I feel it swell me; my revenge is just,        190
I was begot in impudent wine and lust.
Stepmother, I consent to thy desires;
I love thy mischief well, but I hate thee,
And those three cubs, thy sons, wishing confusion,
Death, and disgrace may be their epitaphs.        195
As for my brother, the duke's only son,
Whose birth is more beholding to report
Than mine, and yet perhaps as falsely sown
(Women must not be trusted with their own),
I'll loose my days upon him, hate-all I.        200
Duke, on thy brow I'll draw my bastardy.
For indeed a bastard by nature should make cuckolds,
Because he is the son of a cuckold-maker.        *Exit.*

184. rose] *Dodsley;* rise *Q.*

---

176. arm . . . heraldry] blazon thy dishonor with cuckold's horns.
180. stirring] physically stimulating (*OED*).
188. stol'n] illicitly conceived.
188. met] encountered; with play upon met (a form of "meet"), suitable.
196. duke's] disyllabic; cf. I.i.28, note.
200. loose my days] expend my life in vengeance.

[I.iii]

*Enter* Vindice *and* Hippolito, Vindice *in disguise* [*as Piato*] *to attend* L[*ord*] Lussurioso, *the Duke's son.*

VINDICE.

What, brother, am I far enough from my self?

HIPPOLITO.

As if another man had been sent whole
Into the world, and none wist how he came.

VINDICE.

It will confirm me bold: the child o'th' court;
Let blushes dwell i'th' country. Impudence!       5
Thou goddess of the palace, mistress of mistresses,
To whom the costly-perfum'd people pray,
Strike thou my forehead into dauntless marble,
Mine eyes to steady sapphires; turn my visage,
And if I must needs glow, let me blush inward,       10
That this immodest season may not spy
That scholar in my cheeks, fool bashfulness,
That maid in the old time, whose flush of grace
Would never suffer her to get good clothes.
Our maids are wiser, and are less asham'd;       15
Save Grace the bawd, I seldom hear grace nam'd!

HIPPOLITO.

Nay, brother, you reach out o'th' verge now—'sfoot,

[*Enter* Lussurioso, *attended.*]

The duke's son; settle your looks.

17–18.] *Collins; prose in Q.*

---

13. *That . . . time*] "a version of *nuda Antiquitas,* or *Veritas*" (Harrier).
13–14. *whose . . . clothes*] sarcastically explains why *That maid* would lack a wardrobe in *this immodest season* (l. 11). On the iconographic association of nudity with simplicity, truth, and innocence, see Panofsky, pp. 155 ff.
16. *Save*] except for.
16. *Grace the bawd*] Reference to an actual contemporary bawd has been suspected, but she has not been identified.
17. *verge*] literally, the area around the court subject to the rod (*virga*), i.e., the jurisdiction of the Lord High Steward; hence, "the sphere of the court and all it includes as a concept and jurisdiction" (*OED*). With probable punning sense, "beyond virginity."
17. *'sfoot*] by God's foot.

VINDICE.
    Pray let me not be doubted.        [*He steps aside.*]
HIPPOLITO.
    My lord—
LUSSURIOSO.    Hippolito?—
            [*To Servants.*] Be absent, leave us.   20
                           [*Exit Servants.*]
HIPPOLITO.
    My lord, after long search, wary inquiries,
    And politic siftings, I made choice of yon fellow,
    Whom I guess rare for many deep employments.
    This our age swims within him; and if Time
    Had so much hair, I should take him for Time,   25
    He is so near kin to this present minute.
LUSSURIOSO.
    'Tis enough;
    We thank thee; yet words are but great men's blanks;
    Gold, though it be dumb, does utter the best thanks.
                   [*He gives him money.*]
HIPPOLITO.
    Your plenteous honor. —An exc'lent fellow, my lord.   30
LUSSURIOSO.
    So, give us leave.        [*Exit* Hippolito.]
        Welcome, be not far off;
    We must be better acquainted. Push, be bold
    With us: thy hand.
VINDICE.        With all my heart, i'faith.
    How dost, sweet muskcat? When shall we lie together?
LUSSURIOSO.
    Wondrous knave!            35

31–34.] *Harrier; prose in Q.*

---

   19. *doubted*] suspected, mistrusted.
   24. *Time*] in the sense of Occasion, the present decisive moment; cf.
I.i.55, note.
   25. *Time*] as above, with the additional sense, "the time."
   28. *blanks*] "lottery tickets which do not gain prizes" (Harrison).
   34. *muskcat*] literally, the musk-deer, from which the substance used in
perfumes was got; "by transference a term of reproach for a fop; also
applied to prostitutes" (*OED*).

　　　Gather him into boldness; 'sfoot, the slave's
　　　Already as familiar as an ague,
　　　And shakes me at his pleasure. Friend, I can
　　　Forget myself in private, but elsewhere
　　　I pray do you remember me.

VINDICE.　　　　　　　　　　　O very well, sir.—　　　　40
　　　I conster myself saucy.

LUSSURIOSO.　　　　　　　What hast been?
　　　Of what profession?

VINDICE.　　　　　　A bone-setter.

LUSSURIOSO.　　　　　　　　　A bone-setter!

VINDICE.
　　　A bawd, my lord.
　　　One that sets bones together.

LUSSURIOSO.　　　　　　　　　Notable bluntness!—
　　　[*Aside.*] Fit, fit for me, e'en train'd up to my hand.—　　45
　　　Thou hast been scrivener to much knavery, then.

VINDICE.
　　　Fool to abundance, sir; I have been witness
　　　To the surrenders of a thousand virgins,
　　　And not so little;
　　　I have seen patrimonies wash'd a-pieces,　　　　50
　　　Fruit fields turn'd into bastards,
　　　And in a world of acres,
　　　Not so much dust due to the heir 'twas left to
　　　As would well gravel a petition.

LUSSURIOSO [*aside*].
　　　Fine villain! troth, I like him wonderously.　　　55
　　　He's e'en shap'd for my purpose. —Then thou know'st

47. Fool] *Dodsley;* Foole, Q.　　　53. left to] *Dodsley;* left too Q.

36. *Gather . . . boldness*] This appears to mean "Merely admit him into
your company, and his behavior's at once boldness itself."
　41. *conster*] construe.
　46. *scrivener*] a notary or drawer-up of contracts.
　47. *Fool*] Nicoll suggests this means "voluntary dupe." The term is
invited by *knavery* (l. 46), and distinguishes, in a world "divided into knaves
and fools" (II.ii.5), between knaves who perform it and their agents.
　54. *gravel*] "sand it, to prevent it from blotting while the ink was wet"
(Steevens).

I'th' world strange lust.

VINDICE.                    O Dutch lust! fulsome lust!
Drunken procreation, which begets so many drunkards.
Some father dreads not (gone to bed in wine) to slide
From the mother, and cling the daughter-in-law;                    60
Some uncles are adulterous with their nieces,
Brothers with brothers' wives: O hour of incest!
Any kin now, next to the rim o'th' sister,
Is man's meat in these days; and in the morning,
When they are up and dress'd, and their mask on,                    65
Who can perceive this, save that eternal eye
That sees through flesh and all? Well, if any thing
Be damn'd, it will be twelve o'clock at night;
That twelve will never 'scape;
It is the Judas of the hours, wherein                    70
Honest salvation is betray'd to sin.

LUSSURIOSO.

In troth, it is, too. But let this talk glide.
It is our blood to err, though hell gap'd loud;
Ladies know Lucifer fell, yet still are proud.
Now, sir, wert thou as secret as thou'rt subtle                    75
And deeply fathom'd into all estates,
I would embrace thee for a near employment,
And thou shouldst swell in money, and be able
To make lame beggars crouch to thee.

VINDICE.                    My lord!
Secret? I ne'er had that disease o'th' mother,                    80
I praise my father. Why are men made close
But to keep thoughts in best? I grant you this,
Tell but some woman a secret over night,
Your doctor may find it in the urinal i'th' morning.
But, my lord—

---

60. *cling*] embrace.

63. *rim*] (1) edge; (2) (rim of the) womb (*OED*); (3) chink (Bailey).

80–81. *Secret . . . father*] plays upon the disease called "the mother" (hysteria): "I never suffered the feminine weakness for blabbing, thanks to my father's framing me a man."

81–84. *Why . . . morning*] The thought underlies the somewhat later usage of "leaky" (see Grose).

LUSSURIOSO.                So, thou'rt confirm'd in me,                    85
  And thus I enter thee.                      [*He gives him money.*]
VINDICE.                         This Indian devil
  Will quickly enter any man, but a usurer;
  He prevents that, by ent'ring the devil first.
LUSSURIOSO.
  Attend me. I am past my depth in lust,
  And I must swim or drown. All my desires                  90
  Are levell'd at a virgin not far from court,
  To whom I have convey'd by messenger
  Many wax'd lines, full of my neatest spirit,
  And jewels that were able to ravish her
  Without the help of man; all which and more               95
  She, foolish-chaste, sent back, the messengers
  Receiving frowns for answers.
VINDICE.                              Possible!
  'Tis a rare Phoenix, whoe'er she be.
  If your desires be such, she so repugnant,
  In troth, my lord, I'd be reveng'd and marry her.           100
LUSSURIOSO.
  Push! the dowry of her blood and of her fortunes
  Are both too mean—good enough to be bad withal.
  I'm one of that number can defend
  Marriage is good, yet rather keep a friend.
  Give me my bed by stealth—there's true delight;             105
  What breeds a loathing in't, but night by night?
VINDICE.
  A very fine religion!
LUSSURIOSO.                    Therefore, thus:

---

  86. *enter*] introduce into a condition or state (*OED*).
  86. *Indian devil*] alluding to gold from the Indies, with suggestion, perhaps, of the worship of false gods.
  87. *enter*] diabolically possess.
  88. *prevents*] renders impracticable by anticipatory action; with ironic glance at secondary sense, "keeps from befalling himself" (*OED*).
  93. *wax'd lines*] sealed letters.    93. *neatest*] most cleverly phrased.
  98. *rare Phoenix*] a person of unique excellence, after the mythical bird, fabled to be the only one of its kind (*OED*).
  104. *friend*] paramour.

I'll trust thee in the business of my heart
Because I see thee well experienc'd
In this luxurious day wherein we breathe.                110
Go thou, and with a smooth enchanting tongue
Bewitch her ears, and cozen her of all grace;
Enter upon the portion of her soul,
Her honor, which she calls her chastity,
And bring it into expense; for honesty                115
Is like a stock of money laid to sleep,
Which ne'er so little broke, does never keep.

VINDICE.

You have gi'n't the tang, i'faith, my lord.
Make known the lady to me, and my brain
Shall swell with strange invention; I will move it    120
Till I expire with speaking, and drop down
Without a word to save me; but I'll work—

LUSSURIOSO.

We thank thee, and will raise thee; receive her name:
it is the only daughter to Madame Gratiana, the late widow.

VINDICE [aside].

O, my sister, my sister!

LUSSURIOSO.                 Why dost walk aside?        125

VINDICE.

My lord, I was thinking how I might begin,
As thus, "O lady"—or twenty hundred devices;
Her very bodkin will put a man in.

LUSSURIOSO.

Ay, or the wagging of her hair.

109. experienc'd] *Dodsley;* experi-    112. cozen] *Dodsley;* Couzen *Q.*
enc'st *Q.*

___

112. *cozen*] cheat.
113. *portion*] birthright.
115. *expense*] expenditure; i.e., seduce her to liquidate her soul's inheritance and bring it into use. Cf. I.iii.182.
118. *gi'n't the tang*] given the true taste of it.
122. *Without . . . me*] unable to voice a last-minute repentance.
127. *devices*] witty openings, verbal stratagems.
128. *bodkin*] "a long pin or pin-shaped ornament used by women to
fasten up the hair"; also, "a small pointed instrument . . . used for piercing
holes in cloth, etc." (*OED*).
128. *put . . . in*] afford occasion to speak.

VINDICE.

No, that shall put you in, my lord.                                      130

LUSSURIOSO.

Shall't? why, content. Dost know the daughter then?

VINDICE.

O exc'lent well by sight.

LUSSURIOSO.                           That was her brother

That did prefer thee to us.

VINDICE.                        My lord, I think so;

I knew I had seen him somewhere—

LUSSURIOSO.

And therefore, prithee, let thy heart to him          135

Be as a virgin, close.

VINDICE.                  O, my good lord.

LUSSURIOSO.

We may laugh at that simple age within him—

VINDICE.

Ha, ha, ha.

LUSSURIOSO.

Himself being made the subtle instrument,

To wind up a good fellow—

VINDICE.                    That's I, my lord.          140

LUSSURIOSO.

That's thou—

To entice and work his sister.

VINDICE.                      A pure novice!

LUSSURIOSO.

'Twas finely manag'd.

VINDICE.              Gallantly carried;

A pretty, perfum'd villain.

LUSSURIOSO.                  I've bethought me,

If she prove chaste still and immovable,              145

Venture upon the mother, and with gifts

As I will furnish thee, begin with her.

136. my] *Dodsley;* me *Q.*

---

130. *that*] with obscene reference to "wagging of her hair" (l. 129);
see Partridge, p. 124.
140. *wind . . . fellow*] to set a thief in readiness. Harrison sees a windlass
metaphor in *wind up.*

VINDICE.

O fie, fie! that's the wrong end, my lord. 'Tis mere impossible that a mother by any gifts should become a bawd to
her own daughter!                                                    150

LUSSURIOSO.

Nay, then, I see thou'rt but a puny in the subtle mystery
of a woman.
Why, 'tis held now no dainty dish: the name
Is so in league with age, that nowadays
It does eclipse three quarters of a mother.                          155

VINDICE.

Does't so, my lord?
Let me alone then to eclipse the fourth.

LUSSURIOSO.

Why, well said; come, I'll furnish thee; but first
Swear to be true in all.

VINDICE.                    True!

LUSSURIOSO.                            Nay, but swear!

VINDICE.

Swear?—I hope your honor little doubts my faith.          160

LUSSURIOSO.

Yet for my humor's sake, 'cause I love swearing.

VINDICE.

'Cause you love swearing, 'slud, I will.

LUSSURIOSO.                              Why, enough.

Ere long look to be made of better stuff.

VINDICE.

That will do well indeed, my lord.

LUSSURIOSO [to Servants within].          Attend me!

[Exit Lussurioso.]

VINDICE.

O,                                                                   165
Now let me burst, I've eaten noble poison;
We are made strange fellows, brother, innocent villains.
Wilt not be angry when thou hear'st on't, think'st thou?

153.] Hazlitt; prose in Q.          158–159. Why . . . all] Dodsley;
156. Does't] Collins; Dost Q.          prose in Q.

151. puny] novice.          153. the name] referring to bawd, l. 149.
154. age] the age.          162. 'slud] by God's blood.

I'faith, thou shalt. Swear me to foul my sister!
Sword, I durst make a promise of him to thee;                    170
Thou shalt disheir him, it shall be thine honor.
And yet, now angry froth is down in me,
It would not prove the meanest policy
In this disguise to try the faith of both.
Another might have had the selfsame office,                      175
Some slave, that would have wrought effectually,
Ay, and perhaps o'erwrought 'em; therefore I,
Being thought travel'd, will apply myself
Unto the selfsame form, forget my nature,
As if no part about me were kin to 'em;                          180
So touch 'em—though I durst, almost for good,
Venture my lands in heaven upon their blood.               *Exit.*

[I.iv]
*Enter the discontented* Lord Antonio, *whose wife the Duchess' Youngest
Son ravish'd; he discovering the body of her dead to certain Lords*[, Piero,] *and*
Hippolito.

ANTONIO.

Draw nearer, lords, and be sad witnesses
Of a fair comely building newly fall'n,
Being falsely undermined: violent rape
Has play'd a glorious act. Behold, my lords,
A sight that strikes man out of me.                               5
PIERO.

That virtuous lady!
ANTONIO.                           Precedent for wives!
HIPPOLITO.

The blush of many women, whose chaste presence
Would e'en call shame up to their cheeks,

182. blood] *Dodsley;* good *Q.*

---

172. *froth*] indignation.
181. *touch*] test, try; literally, "test the fineness of (gold or silver) by
rubbing it upon a touchstone" (*OED*).
182. *blood*] here, their "honesty," their incorruptible mastery of lower
nature.
[I.iv]
0.2. *discovering*] revealing.

And make pale wanton sinners have good colors—
ANTONIO.                              Dead!
   Her honor first drunk poison, and her life,                    10
   Being fellows in one house, did pledge her honor.
PIERO.
   O grief of many!
ANTONIO.                    I mark'd not this before:
   A prayer book the pillow to her cheek.
   This was her rich confection; and another
   Plac'd in her right hand, with a leaf tuck'd up,                    15
   Pointing to these words:
   *Melius virtute mori, quam per dedecus vivere.*
   True and effectual it is indeed.
HIPPOLITO.
   My lord, since you invite us to your sorrows,
   Let's truly taste 'em, that with equal comfort,                    20
   As to ourselves, we may relieve your wrongs.
   We have grief too, that yet walks without tongue:
   *Curae leves loquuntur, majores stupent.*
ANTONIO.
   You deal with truth, my lord.
   Lend me but your attentions, and I'll cut                    25
   Long grief into short words. Last reveling night,
   When torchlight made an artificial noon
   About the court, some courtiers in the masque,
   Putting on better faces than their own
   (Being full of fraud and flattery), amongst whom                    30
   The duchess' youngest son (that moth to honor)
   Fill'd up a room; and with long lust to eat

15. Plac'd] *Dodsley;* Plastc'd *Q.*

---

11. *pledge*] gave assurance of fidelity by or in the act of drinking (*OED*).
17. *Melius . . . vivere*] "Better to die in virtue than to live through dishonor" (commonplace, but specific source unknown).
18. *effectual*] pertinent, to the point.
23. *Curae . . . stupent*] "Light cares find speech, greater ones are silent" (from Seneca, *Hippolytus,* 607).
29–30. *better . . . flattery*] In the court masques, courtiers often performed idealized roles symbolically representing the virtues the court was ideally supposed to embody. On masks as commonplace symbols of fraud and deception, see Panofsky, p. 89.
32. *Fill'd up a room*] was one of them.

Into my wearing, amongst all the ladies
Singled out that dear form, who ever liv'd
As cold in lust as she is now in death                                   35
(Which that step-duchess' monster knew too well);
And therefore in the height of all the revels,
When music was heard loudest, courtiers busiest,
And ladies great with laughter—O vicious minute!
Unfit but for relation to be spoke of—                                   40
Then with a face more impudent than his vizard
He harried her amidst a throng of panders,
That live upon damnation of both kinds,
And fed the ravenous vulture of his lust.
O death to think on't! She, her honor forc'd,                            45
Deem'd it a nobler dowry for her name
To die with poison than to live with shame.

HIPPOLITO.

A wondrous lady, of rare fire compact;
Sh'as made her name an empress by that act.

PIERO.

My lord, what judgment follows the offender?                             50

ANTONIO.

Faith, none, my lord; it cools and is deferr'd.

PIERO.

Delay the doom for rape!

ANTONIO.

O, you must note who 'tis should die,
The duchess' son; she'll look to be a saver.
"Judgment in this age is near kin to favor."                             55

36. too] *Dodsley;* to *Q.*          45. forc'd] *Dodsley;* forcst *Q.*
38. heard] *Dodsley;* hard *Q.*

---

33. *wearing*] continuing the *moth* image (l. 31).
42. *harried*] ravished.
43. *damnation*] sin incurring or deserving of damnation (*OED*).
44. *fed . . . lust*] The image is based on a buried allusion to Tityus (one of the four great sinners of Hades), punished for having attacked Latona, mother of Apollo and Diana, by having his liver (producer of blood and therefore seat of the passions) eternally devoured by a vulture. For Renaissance interpretation of the myth "as an allegory of the 'tortures caused by immoderate love,'" see Panofsky, p. 217.
54. *saver*] " a term used in various games" (Nicoll).

HIPPOLITO.

Nay, then, step forth thou bribeless officer.

*[He draws his sword.]*

I bind you all in steel to bind you surely;
Here let your oaths meet, to be kept and paid,
Which else will stick like rust, and shame the blade;
Strengthen my vow, that if at the next sitting                60
Judgment speak all in gold, and spare the blood
Of such a serpent, e'en before their seats
To let his soul out, which long since was found
Guilty in heaven.

ALL.                We swear it and will act it.

*[They swear upon the sword.]*

ANTONIO.

Kind gentlemen, I thank you in mine ire.                65

HIPPOLITO.

'Twere pity
The ruins of so fair a monument
Should not be dipp'd in the defacer's blood.

PIERO.

Her funeral shall be wealthy, for her name
Merits a tomb of pearl. My Lord Antonio,                70
For this time wipe your lady from your eyes;
No doubt our grief and yours may one day court it,
When we are more familiar with revenge.

ANTONIO.

That is my comfort, gentlemen; and I joy
In this one happiness above the rest,                75
Which will be call'd a miracle at last:
That, being an old man, I'd a wife so chaste.                *Exeunt.*


[II.i]                *Enter* Castiza, *the sister* [*of Vindice*].

CASTIZA.

How hardly shall that maiden be beset

68. Should] *Dodsley;* Sould Q.          76. miracle] *Dodsley;* miralce Q.

---

58. *Here*] upon the sword.
[II.i]
    1. *hardly*] severely, with hardship.

Whose only fortunes are her constant thoughts,
That has no other child's-part but her honor,
That keeps her low and empty in estate.
Maids and their honors are like poor beginners;                5
Were not sin rich, there would be fewer sinners.
Why had not virtue a revenue? Well,
I know the cause: 'twould have impoverish'd hell.

[*Enter* Dondolo.]

How now, Dondolo?

DONDOLO.

Madonna, there is one, as they say, a thing of flesh and    10
blood, a man I take him by his beard, that would very
desirously mouth to mouth with you.

CASTIZA.

What's that?

DONDOLO.

Show his teeth in your company.

CASTIZA.

I understand thee not.                                          15

DONDOLO.

Why, speak with you, madonna!

CASTIZA.

Why, say so, madman, and cut off a great deal of dirty
way; had it not been better spoke in ordinary words, that
one would speak with me?

DONDOLO.

Ha, ha, that's as ordinary as two shillings. I would strive    20
a little to show myself in my place; a gentleman-usher
scorns to use the phrase and fancy of a servingman.

CASTIZA.

Yours be your own, sir; go, direct him hither.

[*Exit* Donodolo.]

I hope some happy tidings from my brother,
That lately travel'd, whom my soul affects.                     25
Here he comes.

17. off] *Dodsley;* of *Q*.          23. own] *Dodsley;* one *Q*.

---

3. *child's-part*] child's share of inheritance.
7. *revenue*] accented on second syllable.
25. *affects*] loves.

*Enter* Vindice, *her brother, disguised.*

VINDICE.

Lady, the best of wishes to your sex:
Fair skins and new gowns.

CASTIZA.                    O, they shall thank you, sir.
Whence this?

VINDICE.        O, from a dear and worthy friend,
Mighty!

CASTIZA.        From whom?

VINDICE.                    The duke's son!

CASTIZA.                            Receive that!        30
            *[She gives] a box o'th' ear to her brother.*
I swore I'd put anger in my hand,
And pass the virgin limits of my self
To him that next appear'd in that base office,
To be his sin's attorney. Bear to him
That figure of my hate upon thy cheek            35
Whilst 'tis yet hot, and I'll reward thee for't;
Tell him my honor shall have a rich name
When several harlots shall share his with shame.
Farewell; commend me to him in my hate!        *Exit.*

VINDICE.

It is the sweetest box that e'er my nose came nigh,        40
The finest drawn-work cuff that e'er was worn;
I'll love this blow forever, and this cheek
Shall still henceforward take the wall of this.
O, I'm above my tongue: most constant sister,
In this thou hast right honorable shown;            45

29–30. O .../ Mighty] *Collins;*
*prose in Q.*

---

35. *figure*] image, representation.
41. *drawn-work cuff*] punning on the term for the bottom of a sleeve
ornamented with "work done . . . by drawing out some of the threads of
warp and woof, so as to form patterns"; with reference to *figure* (l. 35) in the
verbal sense, "to trace ( . . . a figure) by drawing . . . [an instrument—here,
a blow with the open hand] across a surface" (*OED*).
43. *take . . . of*] have the privileged position over; from "the right or
privilege of walking next the wall as the cleaner and safer side of a pave-
ment" (*OED*).
45. *right honorable*] truly honorable, playing upon the style of address
"applied to peers below the rank of Marquess, to Privy Councillors, and to
certain civil functionaries" (*OFD*).

Many are call'd by their honor that have none.
Thou art approv'd forever in my thoughts.
It is not in the power of words to taint thee.
And yet for the salvation of my oath,
As my resolve in that point, I will lay                              50
Hard siege unto my mother, though I know
A siren's tongue could not bewitch her so.

[*Enter* Gratiana.]

Mass, fitly here she comes!—Thanks, my disguise.—
Madame, good afternoon.
GRATIANA.                              Y'are welcome, sir.
VINDICE.
The next of Italy commends him to you,                              55
Our mighty expectation, the duke's son.
GRATIANA.
I think myself much honor'd that he pleases
To rank me in his thoughts.
VINDICE.                              So may you, lady:
One that is like to be our sudden duke;
The crown gapes for him every tide, and then                        60
Commander o'er us all. Do but think on him;
How bless'd were they now that could pleasure him,
E'en with anything almost.
GRATIANA.                              Ay, save their honor.
VINDICE.
Tut, one would let a little of that go too,
And ne'er be seen in't: ne'er be seen in't, mark you.               65
I'd wink and let it go—
GRATIANA.                              Marry, but I would not.
VINDICE.
Marry, but I would, I hope; I know you would too,
If you'd that blood now which you gave your daughter.

65. in't,] *Dodsley;* it, *Q.*

---

49. *salvation*] preserving; but the nature of the oath (cf. II.ii.36, 98–99)
and the ironic conception of Vindice's role allow the spiritual sense, "the
saving of the soul," to obtrude.
    50. *resolve*] determination.
    53. *Mass*] by the mass.
    55. *next*] next ruler.

To her indeed 'tis, this wheel comes about;
That man that must be all this, perhaps ere morning          70
(For his white father does but mold away),
Has long desir'd your daughter.
GRATIANA.                                  Desir'd?
VINDICE.
Nay, but hear me:
He desires now that will command hereafter;
Therefore be wise. I speak as more a friend          75
To you than him; madam, I know y'are poor,
And, 'lack the day,
There are too many poor ladies already.
Why should you vex the number? 'tis despis'd.
Live wealthy, rightly understand the world;          80
And chide away that foolish country girl
Keeps company with your daughter, Chastity.
GRATIANA.
O fie, fie! the riches of the world cannot hire
A mother to such a most unnatural task.
VINDICE.
No, but a thousand angels can;          85
Men have no power, angels must work you to't.
The world descends into such base-born evils
That forty angels can make fourscore devils.
There will be fools still, I perceive, still fools.
Would I be poor, dejected, scorn'd of greatness,          90
Swept from the palace, and see other daughters
Spring with the dew o'th' court, having mine own
So much desir'd and lov'd—by the duke's son?
No, I would raise my state upon her breast,
And call her eyes my tenants; I would count          95
My yearly maintenance upon her cheeks,

83–84.] *Mermaid; prose in Q.*          89. still fools] *Hazlitt;* still foole *Q.*

---

69. *wheel*] wheel of fortune.
71. *white*] white-haired; but perhaps also, sardonically, "highly prized,"
on analogy with *white son,* "a beloved or favorite son" (*OED*).
79. *vex*] probably a dialectal form (some eds. suppose an error) for *wax,*
"increase"; with jocular additional sense, "disturb by encroachment."
85. *angels*] play on the name of the English gold coin worth ten shillings.
96. *maintenance*] "the amount provided for a person's livelihood" (*OED*).

Take coach upon her lip and all her parts
Should keep men after men, and I would ride
In pleasure upon pleasure.
You took great pains for her, once when it was;          100
Let her requite it now, though it be but some.
You brought her forth; she may well bring you home.

GRATIANA.
O heavens! this overcomes me!

VINDICE [aside].
Not, I hope, already?

GRATIANA [aside].
It is too strong for me; men know that know us,          105
We are so weak their words can overthrow us.
He touch'd me nearly, made my virtues bate,
When his tongue struck upon my poor estate.

VINDICE [aside].
I e'en quake to proceed, my spirit turns edge.
I fear me she's unmother'd; yet I'll venture.          110
"That woman is all male, whom none can enter."—
What think you now, lady? Speak, are you wiser?
What said advancement to you? Thus it said:
The daughter's fall lifts up the mother's head.
Did it not, madam? But I'll swear it does          115
In many places; tut, this age fears no man.
" 'Tis no shame to be bad, because 'tis common."

GRATIANA.
Ay, that's the comfort on't.

VINDICE.                              The comfort on't!
I keep the best for last; can these persuade you
To forget heaven, and—

                                        [He gives her money.]
GRATIANA.                    Ay, these are they—          120

VINDICE [aside].
O!

---

102. *bring you home*] literal play upon the expression for "recover you
financially."
107. *touch'd me nearly*] tellingly guessed my particular state.
107. *bate*] decline.
111. *enter*] (1) persuade, (2) sexually enter.

GRATIANA.    —That enchant our sex, these are the means
    That govern our affections; that woman
    Will not be troubled with the mother long,
    That sees the comfortable shine of you:
    I blush to think what for your sakes I'll do!              125
VINDICE [*aside*].
    O suff'ring heaven, with thy invisible finger
    E'en at this instant turn the precious side
    Of both mine eyeballs inward, not to see myself.
GRATIANA.
    Look you, sir.
VINDICE.            Holla.
GRATIANA.            Let this thank your pains.    [*She tips him.*]
VINDICE.
    O, you're a kind madam.                                   130
GRATIANA.
    I'll see how I can move.
VINDICE [*aside*].            Your words will sting.
GRATIANA.
    If she be still chaste, I'll ne'er call her mine.
VINDICE [*aside*].
    Spoke truer than you meant it.
GRATIANA [*at one door*].
    Daughter Castiza.

                [*Re-enter Castiza at the other door.*]

CASTIZA.            Madam.
VINDICE.            O, she's yonder;
    Meet her.—                                                135
    [*Aside.*] Troops of celestial soldiers guard her heart.
    Yon dam has devils enough to take her part.

130. madam] *Dodsley;* Mad-man *Q.*

---

123. *the mother*] another play on this as the term for "hysteria" (cf.
I.iii.80–81, note, and II.i.237).

124. *comfortable shine*] comforting shine (assuming the hierarchical gold:
sun correspondence).

126. *suff'ring*] long-suffering.

130. *kind*] with sarcastic covert meaning, "natural, maternal."

134. S.D. *Re-enter . . . door*] The conjectured staging (supported by *she's
yonder*) dramatizes the opposed attitudes of Gratiana and Castiza.

CASTIZA.

  Madam, what makes yon evil-offic'd man
  In presence of you?

GRATIANA.                    Why?

CASTIZA.                         He lately brought
  Immodest writing sent from the duke's son          140
  To tempt me to dishonorable act.

GRATIANA.

  Dishonorable act!—Good honorable fool,
  That wouldst be honest 'cause thou wouldst be so,
  Producing no one reason but thy will.
  And 'tas a good report, prettily commended,        145
  But pray, by whom? mean people, ignorant people;
  The better sort, I'm sure, cannot abide it.
  And by what rule should we square out our lives,
  But by our betters' actions? O, if thou knew'st
  What 'twere to lose it, thou would never keep it.   150
  But there's a cold curse laid upon all maids,
  Whilst others clip the sun, they clasp the shades.
  Virginity is paradise lock'd up.
  You cannot come by your selves without fee,
  And 'twas decreed that man should keep the key!      155
  Deny advancement, treasure, the duke's son!

CASTIZA.

  I cry you mercy, lady, I mistook you.
  Pray, did you see my mother? Which way went you?
  Pray God I have not lost her.

VINDICE [aside].                 Prettily put by.

GRATIANA.

  Are you as proud to me as coy to him?               160
                                        [She slaps her.]
  Do you not know me now?

CASTIZA.                     Why, are you she?
  The world's so chang'd, one shape into another,

148. should] *Dodsley;* shouldst Q.    152. others] *Dodsley;* other Q.

---

140. *duke's*] disyllabic; cf. I.i.28, note.
146. *mean*] socially base.
152. *clip*] embrace.
156. *duke's*] disyllabic; cf. I.i.28, note.

It is a wise child now that knows her mother.
VINDICE [*aside*].
    Most right, i'faith.
GRATIANA.                 I owe your cheek my hand
    For that presumption now, but I'll forget it.                165
    Come, you shall leave those childish 'haviors,
    And understand your time. Fortunes flow to you;
    What, will you be a girl?
    If all fear'd drowning that spy waves ashore,
    Gold would grow rich, and all the merchants poor.            170
CASTIZA.
    It is a pretty saying of a wicked one;
    But methinks now
    It does not show so well out of your mouth;
    Better in his.
VINDICE [*aside*].   Faith, bad enough in both,
    Were I in earnest, as I'll seem no less.—                    175
    I wonder, lady, your own mother's words
    Cannot be taken, nor stand in full force.
    'Tis honesty you urge; what's honesty?
    'Tis but heaven's beggar;
    And what woman is so foolish to keep honesty,                180
    And be not able to keep herself? No,
    Times are grown wiser and will keep less charge.
    A maid that has small portion now intends
    To break up house, and live upon her friends.
    How bless'd are you! You have happiness alone;               185
    Others must fall to thousands, you to one,
    Sufficient in himself to make your forehead
    Dazzle the world with jewels, and petitionary people
    Start at your presence.
GRATIANA.                 O, if I were young,
    I should be ravish'd.
CASTIZA.                 Ay, to lose your honor.                 190
VINDICE.
    'Slid, how can you lose your honor
    To deal with my lord's grace?

---

182. *charge*] expense.    187. *forehead*] cf. I.ii.4, note.
191. *'Slid*] by God's eyelid.

He'll add more honor to it by his title;
Your mother will tell you how.

GRATIANA.                              That I will.

VINDICE.

O, think upon the pleasure of the palace!                    195
Secured ease and state; the stirring meats
Ready to move out of the dishes,
That e'en now quicken when they're eaten;
Banquets abroad by torchlight, musics, sports;
Bareheaded vassals, that had ne'er the fortune            200
To keep on their own hats, but let horns wear 'em;
Nine coaches waiting—hurry, hurry, hurry!

CASTIZA.

Ay, to the devil.

VINDICE [aside].

Ay, to the devil. —[Aloud.] To th' duke, by my faith.

GRATIANA.

Ay, to the duke; daughter, you'd scorn to think          205
O'th' devil and you were there once.

VINDICE [aside].                        True, for most
There are as proud as he for his heart, i'faith.—
Who'd sit at home in a neglected room,
Dealing her short-liv'd beauty to the pictures,
That are as useless as old men, when those               210
Poorer in face and fortune than herself
Walk with a hundred acres on their backs,
Fair meadows cut into green foreparts?—O,
It was the greatest blessing ever happened to woman,
When farmers' sons agreed and met again,                 215

205–207.] *prose in* Q.

---

196. *Secured*] made free from anxiety and care.
196. *stirring*] physically stimulating.
198. *quicken*] (1) rouse, stimulate, (2) become living.
199. *musics*] bands of musicians.
200–201. *Bareheaded . . . hats*] Inferiors "uncovered" in presence of their lords.
201. *horns*] stag-horn hatracks, with play on cuckoldry.    206. *and*] if.
212–213. *Walk . . . foreparts*] satiric allusion to the sale of farms for court-wardrobes (Symonds).
215. *agreed . . . again*] concurred and reassembled (for business).

To wash their hands, and come up gentlemen.
The commonwealth has flourish'd ever since:
Lands that were mete by the rod, that labor's spar'd;
Tailors ride down, and measure 'em by the yard.
Fair trees, those comely foretops of the field,                220
Are cut to maintain head-tires—much untold.
All thrives but Chastity, she lies a-cold.
Nay, shall I come nearer to you? Mark but this:
Why are there so few honest women, but because 'tis the
poorer profession? That's accounted best that's best 225
followed; least in trade, least in fashion; and that's not
honesty, believe it. And do but note the love and dejected
price of it:
Lose but a pearl, we search, and cannot brook it;
But that once gone, who is so mad to look it?                 230
GRATIANA.
     Troth, he says true.
CASTIZA.              False! I defy you both.
I have endur'd you with an ear of fire;
Your tongues have struck hot irons on my face.—
Mother, come from that poisonous woman there.
GRATIANA.
     Where?
CASTIZA.     Do you not see her? She's too inward then.—      235
Slave, perish in thy office!—You heavens, please
Henceforth to make the mother a disease,
Which first begins with me—yet I've outgone you.      *Exit.*
VINDICE [*aside*].
     O angels, clap your wings upon the skies,
     And give this virgin crystal plaudities!                 240
GRATIANA.
     Peevish, coy, foolish!—but return this answer:

218. mete] *Dodsley;* meat *Q.*

---

216. *come up*] rise in position.      218. *mete*] measured.
221. *head-tires*] headdresses.      229. *brook it*] endure the loss.
230. *that*] honesty (l. 227).
238. *outgone*] outdistanced.
240. *crystal*] with the character of the standard type of clearness, here
with reference to the "crystalline heavens" of Ptolemaic cosmology (*OED*).
241. *Peevish*] headstrong, obstinate.

My lord shall be most welcome, when his pleasure
Conducts him this way. I will sway mine own.
Women with women can work best alone.                    *Exit.*
VINDICE.
    Indeed, I'll tell him so.—                           245
    O, more uncivil, more unnatural,
    Than those base-titled creatures that look downward.
    Why does not heaven turn black, or with a frown
    Undo the world? Why does not earth start up
    And strike the sins that tread upon't? O,            250
    Were't not for gold and women, there would be no
        damnation;
    Hell would look like a lord's great kitchen without fire in't.
    But 'twas decreed before the world began,
    That they should be the hooks to catch at man.       *Exit.*

[II.ii]        *Enter* Lussurioso *with* Hippolito, *Vindice's brother.*

LUSSURIOSO.
    I much applaud thy judgment;
    Thou art well read in a fellow,
    And 'tis the deepest art to study man.
    I know this, which I never learnt in schools,
    The world's divided into knaves and fools.           5
HIPPOLITO [*aside*].
    Knave in your face, my lord—behind your back.
LUSSURIOSO.
    And I much thank thee that thou hast preferr'd

---

247. *those . . . downward*] based on the commonplace belief, drawn from
classical (e.g., Plato, *Timaeus*, 90a; Ovid, *Metamorphoses*, I, 81–86) and hexa-
meral literature, in man's upright posture as a symbol of his heaven-given
superiority to the beasts and kinship with the divine. Thus, Du Bartas
describes the unfallen Adam as "Yet, not his Face down to the earth-ward
bending,/ Like Beasts that but regard their belly" (citations from Merritt
Y. Hughes, ed., *Paradise Lost* [N.Y., 1935], p. 238 n. at VII.509).
    252. *Hell . . . in't*] "alluding to the decay of 'hospitality'" (Salingar,
p. 343).
[II.ii]
    6. *Knave . . . back*] I take this whole line to be spoken aside as Hippolito's
comment on his knavish lord's thinking a fool the servant who is making a
fool of him behind his back: "There's a knave in your presence—though
not in your sight."

A fellow of discourse—well mingled;
And whose brain time hath season'd.
HIPPOLITO.                                    True, my lord.
[*Aside.*] We shall find season once, I hope. O villain!          10
To make such an unnatural slave of me; but—

                    [*Enter* Vindice, *disguised.*]
LUSSURIOSO.
Mass, here he comes.
HIPPOLITO [*aside*].
And now shall I have free leave to depart.
LUSSURIOSO.
Your absence, leave us.
HIPPOLITO [*aside*].            Are not my thoughts true?—
[*Apart to* Vindice.]    I must remove, but brother, you may
    stay.                                                          15
Heart, we are both made bawds a new-found way!          *Exit.*
LUSSURIOSO.
Now we're an even number; a third man's dangerous,
Especially her brother; say, be free,
Have I a pleasure toward?
VINDICE.                        O my lord!
LUSSURIOSO.
Ravish me in thine answer; art thou rare?                         20
Hast thou beguil'd her of salvation,
And rubb'd hell o'er with honey? Is she a woman?
VINDICE.
In all but in desire.
LUSSURIOSO.            Then she's in nothing—
I bate in courage now.
VINDICE.                    The words I brought
Might well have made indifferent honest naught.                   25
A right good woman in these days is chang'd
Into white money with less labor far;

---

8. *discourse*] artful conversational power.
16. *Heart*] exclamatory invocation: "God's heart."
24. *bate in courage*] decline in spirit, lustihood.    25. *naught*] immoral.
26–27. *chang'd . . . money*] corrupted for (mere) silver; the violent exchange or transformation image (the state of goodness becoming that which
it is sold for) is characteristically important.

-41-

Many a maid has turn'd to Mahomet
With easier working; I durst undertake,
Upon the pawn and forfeit of my life,                    30
With half those words to flat a Puritan's wife.
But she is close and good; yet 'tis a doubt
By this time. —O, the mother, the mother!

LUSSURIOSO.

I never thought their sex had been a wonder
Until this minute. What fruit from the mother?          35

VINDICE [aside].

Now must I blister my soul: be forsworn,
Or shame the woman that receiv'd me first.
I will be true; thou liv'st not to proclaim;
Spoke to a dying man, shame has no shame.—
My lord.

LUSSURIOSO.   Who's that?

VINDICE.                    Here's none but I, my lord.      40

LUSSURIOSO.

What would thy haste utter?

VINDICE.                    Comfort.

LUSSURIOSO.                 Welcome.

VINDICE.

The maid being dull, having no mind to travel
Into unknown lands, what did me I straight,
But set spurs to the mother? Golden spurs
Will put her to a false gallop in a trice.              45

LUSSURIOSO.

Is't possible that in this the mother should be damn'd before
the daughter?

VINDICE.

O, that's good manners, my lord; the mother for her age
must go foremost, you know.

LUSSURIOSO.

Thou'st spoke that true; but where comes in this comfort?   50

32–33.] *Hazlitt; prose in Q.*          46–47.] *verse in Q* (Ist ... this/ The
                                        ... daughter?)

---

28. *turn'd to Mahomet*] turned "infidel," cant for "become a prostitute"
(cf. "pagan," e.g., in 2 *Henry IV* II.ii.168).
31. *flat*] lay flat.        38. *thou*] i.e., Lussurioso.

VINDICE.

    In a fine place, my lord. —The unnatural mother
Did with her tongue so hard beset her honor,
That the poor fool was struck to silent wonder;
Yet still the maid, like an unlighted taper,
Was cold and chaste, save that her mother's breath      55
Did blow fire on her cheeks. The girl departed,
But the good ancient madam, half mad, threw me
These promising words, which I took deeply note of:
"My lord shall be most welcome—"

LUSSURIOSO.                  Faith, I thank her.

VINDICE.

    —"When his pleasure conducts him this way—"      60

LUSSURIOSO.

    That shall be soon, i'faith.

VINDICE.              —"I will sway mine own—"

LUSSURIOSO.

    She does the wiser; I commend her for't.

VINDICE.

    —"Women with women can work best alone."

LUSSURIOSO.

    By this light, and so they can, give 'em their due; men are
not comparable to 'em.      65

VINDICE.

    No, that's true; for you shall have one woman knit more in
a hour than any man can ravel again in seven and twenty
year.

LUSSURIOSO.

    Now my desires are happy; I'll make 'em freemen now.—
Thou art a precious fellow; faith, I love thee;      70
Be wise and make it thy revenue: beg, leg!
What office couldst thou be ambitious for?

VINDICE.

    Office, my lord! Marry, if I might have my wish, I would
have one that was never begg'd yet.

56. cheeks] *Dodsley;* checkes *Q.*      61. i'faith] *Dodsley;* ifath *Q.*

---

66. *knit*] in the figurative sense, "unite or combine intimately" (*OED*).
67. *ravel*] unravel.
69. *freemen*] possessed of the freedom of a city, borough, etc.
71. *revenue*] accented on second syllable.      71. *leg*] make a leg, bow.

LUSSURIOSO.

Nay, then thou canst have none.                                    75

VINDICE.

Yes, my lord, I could pick out another office yet; nay, and
keep a horse and drab upon't.—

LUSSURIOSO.

Prithee, good bluntness, tell me.

VINDICE.

Why, I would desire but this, my lord: to have all the fees
behind the arras, and all the farthingales that fall plump    80
about twelve o'clock at night upon the rushes.

LUSSURIOSO.

Thou'rt a mad apprehensive knave. Dost think to make any
great purchase of that?

VINDICE.

O, 'tis an unknown thing, my lord; I wonder 'tas been
miss'd so long.                                                   85

LUSSURIOSO.

Well, this night I'll visit her, and 'tis till then
A year in my desires. Farewell.—
                              [To Servants within.] Attend!—
Trust me with thy preferment.                              Exit.

VINDICE.                              My lov'd lord.—

O, shall I kill him o'th' wrong side now? No!
Sword, thou wast never a backbiter yet.                          90
I'll pierce him to his face; he shall die looking upon me.
Thy veins are swell'd with lust; this shall unfill 'em.
Great men were gods, if beggars could not kill 'em.
Forgive me, heaven, to call my mother wicked;
O lessen not my days upon the earth.                             95

---

77. *drab*] mistress.

80. *arras*] tapestry fabric hangings placed around the walls of rooms.

80. *farthingales*] hooped petticoats.

81. *rushes*] "green rushes were commonly employed for strewing on the
floors of apartments" (*OED*).

82. *apprehensive*] witty.

83. *purchase*] gains, especially booty acquired in pillage or thieving (*OED*).

95–96. *lessen . . . her*] referring to doctrine based on Exodus 20:12:
"Honour thy father and thy mother: that thy dayes may be long upon the
land, which the Lord thy God giveth thee." Cf. IV.iv.8.

I cannot honor her; by this, I fear me,
Her tongue has turn'd my sister into use.
I was a villain not to be forsworn
To this our lecherous hope, the duke's son;
For lawyers, merchants, some divines, and all          100
Count beneficial perjury a sin small.
It shall go hard yet, but I'll guard her honor,
And keep the ports sure.

             *[Re-]enter* Hippolito.

HIPPOLITO.              Brother, how goes the world?
I would know news of you, but I have news
To tell you.
VINDICE.        What, in the name of knavery?          105
HIPPOLITO.
Knavery, faith:
This vicious old duke's worthily abus'd;
The pen of his bastard writes him cuckold!
VINDICE.
His bastard?
HIPPOLITO.      Pray, believe it; he and the duchess
By night meet in their linen; they have been seen          110
By stair-foot panders.
VINDICE.         O sin foul and deep!
Great faults are wink'd at when the duke's asleep.

        *[Enter* Spurio *with two* Servants.]

See, see, here comes the Spurio.
HIPPOLITO.           Monstrous luxur!
VINDICE.
Unbrac'd, two of his valiant bawds with him.

---

97. *use*] "employment for sexual purposes" (*OED*).
99. *duke's*] disyllabic; cf. I.i.28, note.
101. *beneficial perjury*] referring to the doctrine justifying equivocation or
lying under oath for a good cause. Cf. *Macbeth* II.iii.7–8.
102. *It . . . but*] "introducing a statement of what will happen unless
prevented by overpowering circumstances" (*OED*).
108. *pen*] *double-entendre*; see Partridge, p. 163.
110. *linen*] i.e., nightdresses.
114. *Unbrac'd*] "with dress or part of dress unfastened or loosened"
(*OED*).

O, there's a wicked whisper; hell is in his ear.        115
Stay, let's observe his passage—
                                    [*They retire out of earshot.*]
SPURIO.

O, but are you sure on't?
SERVANT.

My lord, most sure on't, for 'twas spoke by one
That is most inward with the duke's son's lust,
That he intends within this hour to steal        120
Unto Hippolito's sister, whose chaste life
The mother has corrupted for his use.
SPURIO.

Sweet word, sweet occasion! Faith then, brother,
I'll disinherit you in as short time
As I was when I was begot in haste;        125
I'll damn you at your pleasure: precious deed!
After your lust, O, 'twill be fine to bleed.
Come, let our passing out be soft and wary.
                            *Exeunt* [Spurio *and* Servants].
VINDICE.

Mark! there, there, that step, now to the duchess.
This their second meeting writes the duke cuckold        130
With new additions, his horns newly reviv'd.
Night! thou that look'st like funeral herald's fees
Torn down betimes i'th' morning, thou hang'st fitly
To grace those sins that have no grace at all.
Now 'tis full sea abed over the world:        135
There's juggling of all sides; some that were maids
E'en at sunset are now perhaps i'th' toll-book.
This woman in immodest thin apparel

---

116.1] The conjectured staging is required by the misunderstanding
revealed at l. 129.
    126. *damn . . . pleasure*] cf. *Hamlet* III.iii.90–92.
    128. *soft*] quiet and unobtrusive.
    132. *fees*] "for phease or pheese, which means tatters or hangings . . . . In
this place then it would mean the black frieze put up on the occasion of a
funeral, which remaining for the night was taken down next morning"
(Collins).
    133. *betimes*] at an early hour.        135. *'tis*] i.e., night is.
    137. *toll-book*] "Alluding to the custom of entering horses sold at fairs
in a book called the 'Toll-book'" (Steevens).

Lets in her friend by water; here a dame
Cunning nails leather hinges to a door                    140
To avoid proclamation. Now cuckolds are
A-coining, apace, apace, apace, apace!
And careful sisters spin that thread i'th' night
That does maintain them and their bawds i'th' day!

HIPPOLITO.
You flow well, brother.

VINDICE.                    Pooh, I'm shallow yet,        145
Too sparing and too modest. Shall I tell thee?
If every trick were told that's dealt by night,
There are few here that would not blush outright.

HIPPOLITO.
I am of that belief, too.

VINDICE.                    Who's this comes?

[*Enter* Lussurioso.]

The duke's son up so late?—Brother, fall back,          150
And you shall learn some mischief.          [Hippolito *retires.*]
                    —My good lord.

LUSSURIOSO.
Piato! why, the man I wish'd for! Come,
I do embrace this season for the fittest
To taste of that young lady.

VINDICE [*aside*].                    Heart and hell.

HIPPOLITO [*aside*].
Damn'd villain.

VINDICE [*aside*].    I ha' no way now to cross it,       155
But to kill him.

LUSSURIOSO.    Come, only thou and I.

VINDICE.
My lord, my lord!

LUSSURIOSO.                    Why dost thou start us?

---

139. *friend*] paramour.
    139. *by water*] alluding to London residences with back entrances on the
Thames.
    147. *trick ... dealt*] The card-game senses are sustained by *told*, "coun-
ted," whose other meaning, "revealed," follows *trick* in the senses of "a
bout of love-making; a sexual strategem" (Partridge, p. 208).
    148. *here*] in the audience.          151. *mischief*] evil done on purpose.

VINDICE.

    I'd almost forgot—the bastard!

LUSSURIOSO.                    What of him?

VINDICE.

    This night, this hour, this minute, now—

LUSSURIOSO.                         What? what?

VINDICE.

    —Shadows the duchess—

LUSSURIOSO.                Horrible word.                 160

VINDICE.

    —And like strong poison eats

    Into the duke your father's forehead.

LUSSURIOSO.               O!

VINDICE.

    He makes horn royal.

LUSSURIOSO.           Most ignoble slave!

VINDICE.

    This is the fruit of two beds.

LUSSURIOSO.           I am mad.

VINDICE.

    That passage he trod warily—

LUSSURIOSO.                He did!                     165

VINDICE.

    —And hush'd his villains every step he took.

LUSSURIOSO.

    His villains! I'll confound them.

VINDICE.

    Take 'em finely, finely now.

LUSSURIOSO.

    The duchess' chamber door shall not control me.

                     *Exeunt* [Lussurioso *and* Vindice].

HIPPOLITO.

    Good, happy, swift! There's gunpowder i'th' court,      170

    Wildfire at midnight. In this heedless fury

    He may show violence to cross himself.

    I'll follow the event.                            *Exit.*

---

    164. *fruit . . . beds*] Incest often was regarded the probable consequence of adultery.

    168. *finely*] (1) perfectly, completely; (2) cunningly (*OED*).

[II.iii]

[*The* Duke *and* Duchess *are discovered in bed.*] *Enter again* [Lussurioso *and* Vindice *disguised*].

LUSSURIOSO.

Where is that villain?

VINDICE.

Softly, my lord, and you may take 'em twisted.

LUSSURIOSO.

I care not how!

VINDICE.                    O, 'twill be glorious

To kill 'em doubled, when they're heap'd. Be soft, my lord.

LUSSURIOSO.

Away, my spleen is not so lazy; thus and thus          5

I'll shake their eyelids ope, and with my sword

Shut 'em again forever.          [*He approaches the bed.*]

                    —Villain! strumpet!

DUKE.

You upper guard, defend us!

DUCHESS.                    Treason, treason!

DUKE.

O take me not in sleep!

I have great sins; I must have days,          10

Nay, months, dear son, with penitential heaves,

To lift 'em out, and not to die unclear.

O, thou wilt kill me both in heaven and here.

LUSSURIOSO.

I am amaz'd to death.

DUKE.                    Nay, villain traitor,

Worse than the foulest epithet, now I'll gripe thee          15

E'en with the nerves of wrath, and throw thy head

Amongst the lawyers!—Guard!

0.1–0.2.] *Harrier;* "*Enter again*" *in*          17. lawyers!—Guard!]          *Collins;*
*margin after l. 1 in Q.*          Lawyers gard *Q.*
4. they're] *Dodsley;* their *Q.*

---

5. *spleen*] Impulsive behavior, such as passionate anger, was supposed due to the action of the spleen.

11. *heaves*] sighs.

12. *unclear*] tainted with sin.

16. *nerves*] sinews.

*Enter* Nobles *and sons* [Ambitioso *and* Supervacuo, Hippolito
*following*].

FIRST NOBLE.

How comes the quiet of your grace disturb'd?

DUKE.

This boy, that should be my self after me,
Would be my self before me, and in heat                       20
Of that ambition bloodily rush'd in,
Intending to depose me in my bed!

SECOND NOBLE.

Duty and natural loyalty forfend!

DUCHESS.

He call'd his father villain; and me strumpet,
A word that I abhor to file my lips with.                     25

AMBITIOSO.

That was not so well done, brother.

LUSSURIOSO [*aside*].

I am abus'd—
I know there's no excuse can do me good.

VINDICE [*apart to* Hippolito].

'Tis now good policy to be from sight.
His vicious purpose to our sister's honor                     30
Is cross'd beyond our thought.

HIPPOLITO [*apart to* Vindice].        You little dreamt
His father slept here.

VINDICE [*apart to* Hippolito]. O, 'twas far beyond me.
But since it fell so—without frightful word,
Would he had kill'd him; 'twould have eas'd our swords.

                       [Vindice *and* Hippolito *slip away*.]

DUKE.

Be comforted, our duchess, he shall die.                      35

LUSSURIOSO [*aside*].

Where's this slave-pander now? out of mine eye,
Guilty of this abuse.

18. grace] *Dodsley;* Gtace *Q.*       34.1.] *Q has marginal S.D.* "dis-
                                        semble a| flight," *beside ll. 35–36.*

---

25. *abhor*] paranomasia; cf. *Othello* IV.ii.162.       25. *file*] defile.
27. *abus'd*] imposed upon, misguided.
29. *policy*] "prudence in the management of affairs" (Onions).
37. *abuse*] imposition.

*Enter* Spurio *with his villains.*

SPURIO.                    Y'are villains, fablers!
You have knaves' chins and harlots' tongues; you lie,
And I will damn you with one meal a day.

FIRST SERVANT.
O good my lord!

SPURIO.                    'Sblood, you shall never sup.          40

SECOND SERVANT.
O, I beseech you, sir!

SPURIO.                    To let my sword
Catch cold so long, and miss him.

FIRST SERVANT.                    Troth, my lord,
'Twas his intent to meet there.

SPURIO.                    Heart, he's yonder.
Ha, what news here? Is the day out o'th' socket,
That it is noon at midnight? the court up?          45
How comes the guard so saucy with his elbows?

LUSSURIOSO [*aside*].
The bastard here?
Nay, then the truth of my intent shall out.—
My lord and father, hear me.

DUKE.                    Bear him hence.

LUSSURIOSO.
I can with loyalty excuse—          50

DUKE.
Excuse?—To prison with the villain!
Death shall not long lag after him.

SPURIO [*aside*].
Good, i'faith: then 'tis not much amiss.

LUSSURIOSO.
Brothers, my best release lies on your tongues;
I pray, persuade for me.          55

AMBITIOSO.
It is our duties; make yourself sure of us.

SUPERVACUO.
We'll sweat in pleading.

---

37. *fablers*] liars.

LUSSURIOSO.                    And I may live to thank you.

*Exeunt* [Lussurioso *and Guards*].

AMBITIOSO [*aside*].

No, thy death shall thank me better.

SPURIO [*aside*].

He's gone; I'll after him,
And know his trespass, seem to bear a part                    60
In all his ills, but with a Puritan heart.

*Exit* [Spurio, *with his villains*].

AMBITIOSO [*apart to* Supervacuo].

Now, brother, let our hate and love be woven
So subtly together, that in speaking
One word for his life, we may make three for his death.
The craftiest pleader gets most gold for breath.            65

SUPERVACUO [*apart to* Ambitioso].

Set on, I'll not be far behind you, brother.

DUKE.

Is't possible a son should be disobedient as far as the sword?
It is the highest; he can go no farther.

AMBITIOSO.

My gracious lord, take pity—

DUKE.                         Pity, boys?

AMBITIOSO.

Nay, we'd be loath to move your grace too much;             70
We know the trespass is unpardonable,
Black, wicked, and unnatural.

SUPERVACUO.

In a son, O monstrous!

AMBITIOSO.                 Yet, my lord,
A duke's soft hand strokes the rough head of law,
And makes it lie smooth.

DUKE.                      But my hand shall ne'er do't.      75

AMBITIOSO.

That as you please, my lord.

SUPERVACUO.                   We must needs confess,
Some father would have enter'd into hate
So deadly pointed, that before his eyes

---

61. *Puritan*] i.e., hypocritical.
70. *move*] (1) anger; and, covertly, (2) persuade.

He would ha' seen the execution sound,
Without corrupted favor.

AMBITIOSO.                    But, my lord,                    80
Your grace may live the wonder of all times,
In pard'ning that offence which never yet
Had face to beg a pardon.

DUKE.                    Honey, how's this?

AMBITIOSO.
Forgive him, good my lord; he's your own son,
And I must needs say 'twas the vildlier done.                    85

SUPERVACUO.
He's the next heir; yet this true reason gathers,
None can possess that dispossess their fathers.
Be merciful—

DUKE [aside].                    Here's no stepmother's wit;
I'll try 'em both upon their love and hate.

AMBITIOSO.
Be merciful, although—

DUKE.                    You have prevail'd.                    90
My wrath, like flaming wax, hath spent itself.
I know 'twas but some peevish moon in him;
Go, let him be releas'd.

SUPERVACUO [apart to Ambitioso].    'Sfoot, how now, brother?

AMBITIOSO.
Your grace doth please to speak beside your spleen;
I would it were so happy.

DUKE.                    Why, go, release him.                    95

SUPERVACUO.
O, my good lord, I know the fault's too weighty
And full of general loathing, too inhumane,
Rather by all men's voices worthy death.

DUKE.
'Tis true too.
Here, then, receive this signet: doom shall pass.                    100

---

79. *sound*] thoroughly, unimpairedly performed.
85. *vildlier*] more vilely.
86. *this . . . gathers*] true reason concludes this.
92. *peevish moon*] senseless, capricious frenzy.
94. *spleen*] fit of temper, indignation (*OED*).
100. *signet*] "a small seal . . . employed to give authentication or authority" (*OED*)—here, to a verbal order.

Direct it to the judges; he shall die
Ere many days. Make haste.
AMBITIOSO.                          All speed that may be.
We could have wish'd his burden not so sore;
We knew your grace did but delay before.

                              *Exeunt* [Ambitioso *and* Supervacuo].
DUKE.
Here's envy with a poor thin cover o'er't,                    105
Like scarlet hid in lawn, easily spied through.
This their ambition by the mother's side
Is dangerous, and for safety must be purg'd.
I will prevent their envies; sure it was
But some mistaken fury in our son,                           110
Which these aspiring boys would climb upon.
He shall be releas'd suddenly.

                    *Enter* Nobles.

FIRST NOBLE.
Good morning to your grace.
DUKE.                          Welcome, my lords.
SECOND NOBLE.
Our knees shall take away
The office of our feet forever,                              115
Unless your grace bestow a father's eye
Upon the clouded fortunes of your son,
And in compassionate virtue grant him that
Which makes e'en mean men happy—liberty.
DUKE.
How seriously their loves and honors woo                     120
For that which I am about to pray them do,
Which—rise, my lords—your knees sign: his release.
We freely pardon him.
FIRST NOBLE.
We owe your grace much thanks, and he much duty.

                              *Exeunt* [Nobles].

105. o'er't] *Collier;* or't *Q*.          122. sign:] signe *Q*.

---

105. *envy*] ill-will.
106. *lawn*] fine linen cloth.
112. *suddenly*] (1) unexpectedly, (2) in a very short time.

DUKE.

It well becomes that judge to nod at crimes,          125
That does commit greater himself, and lives.
I may forgive a disobedient error,
That expect pardon for adultery,
And in my old days am a youth in lust.
Many a beauty have I turn'd to poison          130
In the denial, covetous of all.
Age hot is like a monster to be seen:
My hairs are white, and yet my sins are green.          [*Exit.*]

[III.i]                    *Enter* Ambitioso *and* Supervacuo.

SUPERVACUO.

Brother, let my opinion sway you once;
I speak it for the best, to have him die
Surest and soonest; if the signet come
Unto the judges' hands, why then his doom
Will be deferr'd till sittings and court-days,          5
Juries and further. Faiths are bought and sold;
Oaths in these days are but the skin of gold.

AMBITIOSO.

In troth, 'tis true too.

SUPERVACUO.                    Then let's set by the judges
And fall to the officers. 'Tis but mistaking
The duke our father's meaning, and where he nam'd          10
"Ere many days"—'tis but forgetting that,
And have him die i'th' morning.

AMBITIOSO.                    Excellent!
Then am I heir—duke in a minute.

SUPERVACUO [*aside*].                    Nay,
And he were once puff'd out, here is a pin
Should quickly prick your bladder.

AMBITIOSO.                    Bless'd occasion!          15
He being pack'd, we'll have some trick and wile

15. Bless'd] *Dodsley;* Blast *Q.*

---

131. *In the denial*] when she denied me.
[III.i]
  8. *set by*] put on one side, disregard.
  9. *fall to*] apply ourselves to, begin upon.          14. *pin*] i.e., his sword.

To wind our younger brother out of prison,
That lies in for the rape. The lady's dead,
And people's thoughts will soon be buried.

SUPERVACUO.

We may with safety do't, and live and feed;                    20
The duchess' sons are too proud to bleed.

AMBITIOSO.

We are, i'faith, to say true. —Come, let's not linger.
I'll to the officers; go you before,
And set an edge upon the executioner.

SUPERVACUO.

Let me alone to grind him.                              *Exit.*

AMBITIOSO.                    Meet; farewell.—          25
I am next now; I rise just in that place
Where thou'rt cut off, upon thy neck, kind brother;
The falling of one head lifts up another.              *Exit.*

[III.ii]      *Enter with the* Nobles, Lussurioso *from prison.*

LUSSURIOSO.

My lords, I am so much indebted to your loves
For this, O, this delivery—

FIRST NOBLE.                    But our duties,
My lord, unto the hopes that grow in you.

LUSSURIOSO.

If e'er I live to be my self, I'll thank you.
O liberty, thou sweet and heavenly dame!                5
But hell for prison is too mild a name.                 *Exeunt.*

[III.iii]      *Enter* Ambitioso *and* Supervacuo *with* Officers.

AMBITIOSO.

Officers, here's the duke's signet, your firm warrant,
Brings the command of present death along with it
Unto our brother, the duke's son; we are sorry
That we are so unnaturally employ'd
In such an unkind office, fitter far                    5

---

24. *set . . . upon*] make keen (literally and figuratively).
24. *executioner*] playing upon the sense, "instrument of execution."
[III.ii]
2. *But*] only.

For enemies than brothers.

SUPERVACUO.                    But, you know,
The duke's command must be obey'd.

FIRST OFFICER.
It must and shall, my lord—this morning then,
So suddenly?

AMBITIOSO.          Ay, alas! poor, good soul,
He must breakfast betimes; the executioner                    10
Stands ready to put forth his cowardly valor.

SECOND OFFICER.
Already?

SUPERVACUO.
Already, i'faith, O sir, destruction hies;
And that is least imprudent, soonest dies.

FIRST OFFICER.
Troth, you say true, my lord; we take our leaves.          15
Our office shall be sound; we'll not delay
The third part of a minute.

AMBITIOSO.                    Therein you show
Yourselves good men and upright officers.
Pray, let him die as private as he may;
Do him that favor, for the gaping people                    20
Will but trouble him at his prayers
And make him curse and swear, and so die black.
Will you be so far kind?

FIRST OFFICER.                    It shall be done, my lord.

AMBITIOSO.
Why, we do thank you; if we live to be,
You shall have a better office.

SECOND OFFICER.                    Your good lordship.          25

SUPERVACUO.
Commend us to the scaffold in our tears.

FIRST OFFICER.
We'll weep, and do your commendations.          *Exeunt* [Officers].

13. Already, i'faith] *Dodsley;* Al-      14. imprudent] *Hazlitt;* Impudent
reardy ifath Q.                          Q.

---

14. *that . . . imprudent*] i.e., he that is most farsighted.
16. *sound*] thoroughly performed.
22. *black*] impenitent, out of the state of grace.

AMBITIOSO.

Fine fools in office!

SUPERVACUO.          Things fall out so fit!

AMBITIOSO.

So happily! Come, brother, ere next clock
His head will be made serve a bigger block.          *Exeunt.*     30

[III.iv]

*Enter in prison [the Duchess'* Youngest Son *and his* Keeper].

YOUNGEST SON.

Keeper.

KEEPER.          My lord.

YOUNGEST SON.          No news lately from our brothers?
Are they unmindful of us?

KEEPER.

My lord, a messenger came newly in
And brought this from 'em.          [*He gives him a letter.*]

YOUNGEST SON.                    Nothing but paper comforts?
I look'd for my delivery before this,                              5
Had they been worth their oaths. —Prithee, be from us.
                                   [*Exit* Keeper.]
Now, what say you, forsooth? Speak out, I pray.
([*He reads the*] *letter.*) "Brother, be of good cheer."
'Slud, it begins like a whore with good cheer.
"Thou shalt not be long a prisoner."                            10
Not five and thirty year, like a bankrout—
I think so.
"We have thought upon a device to get thee out by a trick."
By a trick!
Pox o' your trick and it be so long a-playing.                  15
"And so rest comforted, be merry and expect it suddenly."
Be merry! Hang merry, draw and quarter merry!
I'll be mad. [*He tears up the letter.*] Is't not strange that a
man should lie in a whole month for a woman? Well, we
shall see how sudden our brothers will be in their promise.    20

_____

30. *block*] the headsman's, with a play on the meaning "hat."
[III.iv]
   11. *bankrout*] bankrupt.
   20. *sudden*] "swift or speedy in action" (Onions).

I must expect still a trick!
I shall not be long a prisoner.

[*Re-enter* Keeper.]

     —How now, what news?

KEEPER.
Bad news, my lord, I am discharg'd of you.

YOUNGEST SON.
Slave, call'st thou that bad news?— [*Aside.*] I thank you,
 brothers.

KEEPER.
My lord, 'twill prove so; here come the officers          25
Into whose hands I must commit you.

[*Enter* Officers.]

YOUNGEST SON.     Ha?
Officers! what? why?

FIRST OFFICER.    You must pardon us, my lord,
Our office must be sound. Here is our warrant,
The signet from the duke: you must straight suffer.

YOUNGEST SON.
Suffer? I'll suffer you to be gone; I'll suffer you          30
To come no more. What would you have me suffer?

SECOND OFFICER.
My lord, those words were better chang'd to prayers;
The time's but brief with you; prepare to die.

YOUNGEST SON.
Sure 'tis not so.

THIRD OFFICER.  It is too true, my lord.

YOUNGEST SON.
I tell you 'tis not, for the duke my father          35
Deferr'd me till next sitting, and I look
E'en every minute threescore times an hour
For a release, a trick wrought by my brothers.

FIRST OFFICER.
A trick, my lord? If you expect such comfort,
Your hope's as fruitless as a barren woman;          40
Your brothers were the unhappy messengers

22.] *prose in* Q.
_____

 21. *still*] (1) yet; and (2) ever.  28. *sound*] thoroughly performed.

That brought this powerful token for your death.

YOUNGEST SON.

My brothers? no, no.

SECOND OFFICER.                'Tis most true, my lord.

YOUNGEST SON.

My brothers to bring a warrant for my death?
How strange this shows!

THIRD OFFICER.                There's no delaying time.          45

YOUNGEST SON.

Desire 'em hither, call 'em up, my brothers!
They shall deny it to your faces.

FIRST OFFICER.                My lord,
They're far enough by this, at least at court;
And this most strict command they left behind 'em.
When grief swum in their eyes, they show'd like brothers,     50
Brimful of heavy sorrow; but the duke
Must have his pleasure.

YOUNGEST SON.                His pleasure!

FIRST OFFICER.

These were their last words which my memory bears:
"Commend us to the scaffold in our tears."

YOUNGEST SON.

Pox dry their tears! What should I do with tears?             55
I hate 'em worse than any citizen's son
Can hate salt water. Here came a letter now,
New-bleeding from their pens, scarce stinted yet—
Would I'd been torn in pieces when I tore it.

                        [*He pieces the letter together.*]

Look you officious whoresons, words of comfort:             60
"Not long a prisoner."

FIRST OFFICER.

It says true in that, sir, for you must suffer presently.

YOUNGEST SON.

A villainous Duns upon the letter, knavish exposition. Look

---

63. *Duns*] interpretation, punningly alluding to Duns Scotus who subtly
"commented upon 'The Master of the Sentences'" (Pegge).

63. *upon the letter*] with punning reference to "literal" interpretation of
a text, the expounding of "the sense which does not go beyond the strict
limits of the letter" (Dante, *Convivio*).

you then here, sir: "We'll get thee out by a trick," says
he.                                                                              65

SECOND OFFICER.
That may hold too, sir, for you know a trick is commonly
four cards, which was meant by us four officers.

YOUNGEST SON.
Worse and worse dealing.

FIRST OFFICER.                    The hour beckons us,
The headsman waits; lift up your eyes to heaven.

YOUNGEST SON.
I thank you, faith; good, pretty-wholesome counsel!          70
I should look up to heaven, as you said,
Whilst he behind me cozens me of my head.
Ay, that's the trick.

THIRD OFFICER.                    You delay too long, my lord.

YOUNGEST SON.
Stay, good Authority's bastards; since I must
Through brothers' perjury die, O let me venom          75
Their souls with curses.

FIRST OFFICER.                    Come, 'tis no time to curse.

YOUNGEST SON.
Must I bleed then, without respect of sign? Well—
My fault was sweet sport, which the world approves;
I die for that which every woman loves.          *Exeunt.*

[III.v]     *Enter* Vindice [*disguised*] *with* Hippolito *his brother.*

VINDICE.
O sweet, delectable, rare, happy, ravishing!

HIPPOLITO.
Why, what's the matter, brother?

VINDICE.                    O, 'tis able
To make a man spring up, and knock his forehead
Against yon silver ceiling.

HIPPOLITO.                    Prithee, tell me;

71. said] *Dodsley;* sedd *Q*.                    4. ceiling] *Dodsley;* seeling *Q*.

---

66–67. *trick . . . cards*] in the game of primero (Collins).
77. *bleed . . . sign*] Therapeutic bleeding was supposed to be done under
favorable astrological *signs*, i.e., conditions (Harrison).
78. *sport*] cf. I.ii.66, note.

Why may not I partake with you? You vow'd once          5
To give me share to every tragic thought.

VINDICE.

By th' mass, I think I did too;
Then I'll divide it to thee. The old duke,
Thinking my outward shape and inward heart
Are cut out of one piece (for he that prates his secrets,          10
His heart stands o'th' outside), hires me by price
To greet him with a lady
In some fit place veil'd from the eyes o'th' court,
Some darken'd blushless angle, that is guilty
Of his forefathers' lusts and great folks' riots;          15
To which I easily (to maintain my shape)
Consented, and did wish his impudent grace
To meet her here in this unsunned lodge,
Wherein 'tis night at noon; and here the rather
Because, unto the torturing of his soul,          20
The bastard and the duchess have appointed
Their meeting too in this luxurious circle;
Which most afflicting sight will kill his eyes
Before we kill the rest of him.

HIPPOLITO.

'Twill, i'faith! Most dreadfully digested!          25
I see not how you could have miss'd me, brother.

VINDICE.

True, but the violence of my joy forgot it.

HIPPOLITO.

Ay, but where's that lady now?

VINDICE.                                        O, at that word

16. I easily (to] *Dodsley;* (I easily
to *Q.*

---

8. *divide it to thee*] deal out your share.

9. *shape*] (1) distinctive visible form; with the additional meanings (2)
assumed appearance, disguise; (3) the theatrical senses: "a part, a character
impersonated; the make-up and costume suited to a particular part; . . . a
stage dress or suit of clothes" (*OED*).

11. *His . . . outside*] i.e., he wears his heart on his sleeve (Nicoll).

15. *riots*] dissolute revels.

25. *digested*] "disposed in or reduced to order" (*OED*).

26. *miss'd me*] failed to meet with me; here (apparently), "failed to let
me in on your plans."

27. *forgot it*] i.e., led me "to drop the practice of" (Onions) that duty.

I'm lost again; you cannot find me yet;
I'm in a throng of happy apprehensions.                    30
He's suited for a lady; I have took care
For a delicious lip, a sparkling eye—
You shall be witness, brother.
Be ready; stand with your hat off.                    *Exit.*

HIPPOLITO.
Troth, I wonder what lady it should be?                    35
Yet 'tis no wonder, now I think again,
To have a lady stoop to a duke, that stoops unto his men.
'Tis common to be common through the world:
And there's more private common shadowing vices
Than those who are known both by their names and prices.   40
'Tis part of my allegiance to stand bare
To the duke's concubine; and here she comes.

[*Re-*]*enter* Vindice, *with the* [*masked*] *skull of his love dress'd up in tires.*

VINDICE [*addressing the skull*].
Madame, his grace will not be absent long.—
Secret? ne'er doubt us, madame. 'Twill be worth
Three velvet gowns to your ladyship. —Known?          45
Few ladies respect that disgrace: a poor thin shell!
'Tis the best grace you have to do it well.
I'll save your hand that labor, I'll unmask you!

HIPPOLITO.
Why brother, brother!

VINDICE.
Art thou beguil'd now? Tut, a lady can,                    50
At such all hid, beguile a wiser man.

31. suited] *Dodsley;* suted *Q.*          46. that disgrace:] *Dodsley;* that?
                                            disgrace, *Q.*

---

30. *apprehensions*] inventive thoughts.

38. *common*] playing on the senses (1) prevalent, and (2) available for public use, i.e., prostituted.

42.1. *tires*] headdresses.

45. *your ladyship*] sarcastic; here, virtually, "your whorship."

50. *beguil'd*] (1) cheated, disappointed; (2) had your attention diverted "in some pleasant way from (anything unpleasant)" (Onions).

51. *all hid*] "the game of Hide-and-Seek (from the words called out by the hiding party)" (*OED*).

Have I not fitted the old surfeiter
With a quaint piece of beauty? Age and bare bone
Are e'er allied in action. Here's an eye,
Able to tempt a great man—to serve God;                      55
A pretty hanging lip, that has forgot now to dissemble;
Methinks this mouth should make a swearer tremble,
A drunkard clasp his teeth and not undo 'em
To suffer wet damnation to run through 'em.
Here's a cheek keeps her color, let the wind go whistle;     60
Spout rain, we fear thee not; be hot or cold,
All's one with us. And is not he absurd,
Whose fortunes are upon their faces set,
That fear no other god but wind and wet?

HIPPOLITO.

Brother, y'ave spoke that right.                             65
Is this the form that, living, shone so bright?

VINDICE.

The very same.
And now methinks I could e'en chide myself
For doting on her beauty, though her death
Shall be reveng'd after no common action.—                   70
Does the silkworm expend her yellow labors
For thee? for thee does she undo herself?

62. absurd] *Dodsley;* absur'd *Q.*          68. could] *Reed;* cold *Q.*

---

53. *quaint piece*] a (1) cleverly appropriate, (2) cunningly contrived,
(3) "skillfully made, so as to have a good appearance; hence . . . fine,
dainty," (4) elegant *piece,* i.e., masterpiece (*OED*); with a sardonic sense,
"cunning piece," playing on the sexual senses of both words.

60. *color*] alluding to the contemporary feminine fashion of painting the
face.

63. *set*] staked.

71. *expend*] lay out, spend; and, connotatively, consume in outlay.

71. *yellow*] figuratively applying the word as used "of the complexion in
age or disease" (*OED*).

72. *For*] intensively and complexly used throughout the passage; here,
in the senses (1) "with the purpose or result of benefiting or gratifying; as a
service to. Also *ironically*"; (2) "indicating the object to which the activity
of the faculties or the feelings is directed" (*OED*).

72. *for*] (1) "in exchange for, as the price of"; (2) sense 2 above; (3) "for
the purpose of being or becoming" (*OED*).

72. *undo*] (1) "ruin, destroy in respect of means or position"; (2) "bring
to naught, do away with" (*OED*), in a sense concordant with the "silkworm's" expense of herself.

Are lordships sold to maintain ladyships
For the poor benefit of a bewitching minute?
Why does yon fellow falsify highways,                    75
And put his life between the judge's lips,
To refine such a thing, keeps horse and men
To beat their valors for her?
Surely we're all mad people, and they
Whom we think are, are not: we mistake those;          80
'Tis we are mad in sense, they but in clothes.

HIPPOLITO.
Faith, and in clothes too we, give us our due.

81. sense] *Dodsley;* scence *Q.*

---

73. *lordships*] the lands or territories of lords; but also with reference to
the sense "the dignity and functions of lords and their domains."
73. *maintain*] (1) pay for the keeping up of; (2) cause (a person) to con-
tinue in the specified state; (3) "preserve (a state of things)" (*OED*).
73. *ladyships*] sarcastic: (1) those in the condition of being a lady; (2)
"whoreships" (the transformation being from *lordships* to whoredoms).
74. *For*] (1) as the price of; (2) in order to obtain.
74. *benefit*] (1) kindness, favor; (2) advantage, profit, good; (3) with the
possibility of *for the benefit of* in the sense, "for the advantage of, in behalf
of" (*OED*).
74. *bewitching minute*] with a literal edge: that (merely, but decisively,
"charming" one) in which a spiritually seduced soul is sold or exchanged
for illusory gain.
75. *yon fellow*] the imagined highwayman, but referring through his
image to the Duke and all the others of Vindice's world who *falsify highways.*
75. *falsify highways*] i.e., act the highwayman; but *falsify* signifies (1)
adulterate, (2) "alter or pervert from correct rule"; and *highways*, as well
as (1) principal public roads, (2) "a course of conduct leading directly
to some end or result" (*OED*).
76. *life . . . lips*] the meaning includes: his spiritual life between the lips
of the Last Judge.
77. *refine*] with original force figuratively applied: "to purify or separate
(metals) from dross," "to free from impurities" (*OED*).
78. *beat*] complexly fuses near-homonymic puns on *beat, bate* (aphetic
form of *abate*), and *bait. Beat,* (1) to strike, or impel, with repeated blows,
(2) overcome, (3) drive by blows; *bate,* (1) to degrade, (2) bring down in
value or force; *bait,* to worry, harrass, with persistent attacks (*OED*).
78. *valors*] (1) intrinsic worth or merit; (2) "the amount in money, etc.
that a thing is worth"; (3) courage, bravery (and here, by extension,
"manhood") (*OED*).
78. *for*] cf. l. 72, note on *For.*
81. *in sense . . . clothes*] i.e., we are mad in our senses, our reasons, they
(by comparison) but in their outward show.

VINDICE.

Does every proud and self-affecting dame
Camphire her face for this? and grieve her Maker
In sinful baths of milk, when many an infant starves,          85
For her superfluous outside—all for this?—
Who now bids twenty pound a night, prepares
Music, perfumes, and sweetmeats?—All are hush'd;
Thou may'st lie chaste now! It were fine, methinks,
To have thee seen at revels, forgetful feasts,          90
And unclean brothels; sure, 'twould fright the sinner
And make him a good coward, put a reveler
Out of his antic amble,
And cloy an epicure with empty dishes.
Here might a scornful and ambitious woman          95
Look through and through herself. —See, ladies, with false
    forms
You deceive men, but cannot deceive worms.—
Now to my tragic business. Look you, brother,
I have not fashion'd this only for show
And useless property; no, it shall bear a part          100
E'en in it own revenge. This very skull,
Whose mistress the duke poisoned, with this drug,
The mortal curse of the earth, shall be reveng'd
In the like strain, and kiss his lips to death.
As much as the dumb thing can, he shall feel;          105
What fails in poison, we'll supply in steel.

HIPPOLITO.

Brother, I do applaud thy constant vengeance,
The quaintness of thy malice, above thought.

                    [Vindice *poisons the mouth of the skull.*]

93. of] *Dodsley;* off *Q.*

---

84. *Camphire*] "to impregnate or wash with camphor" (*OED*) for cos-
metic purposes.
86. *superfluous*] (1) "having, consuming, or expending more than enough";
(2) "that is not needed or required"; (3) "that exceeds what is sufficient"
(*OED*).
100. *property*] (1) the theatrical sense: a stage requisite; and (2) the
figurative sense, "a mere means to an end" (*OED*).
101. *it*] its.

VINDICE.

So, 'tis laid on: now come and welcome, duke,
I have her for thee. —I protest it, brother,          110
Methinks she makes almost as fair a fine
As some old gentlewoman in a periwig.—
[*To the skull.*] Hide thy face now for shame; thou hadst need
    have a mask now.
'Tis vain when beauty flows, but when it fleets,
This would become graves better than the streets.          115

HIPPOLITO.

You have my voice in that.          [*Voices within.*]
                    Hark, the duke's come.

VINDICE.

Peace, let's observe what company he brings,
And how he does absent 'em; for you know
He'll wish all private. —Brother, fall you back a little
With the bony lady.

HIPPOLITO.          That I will.          [*He retires.*]

VINDICE.                    So, so—          120
Now nine years' vengeance crowd into a minute!

                [*Enter the* Duke *and* Gentlemen.]

DUKE.

You shall have leave to leave us, with this charge,
Upon your lives, if we be miss'd by th' duchess
Or any of the nobles, to give out
We're privately rid forth.

VINDICE [*aside*].          O happiness!          125

DUKE.

With some few honorable gentlemen, you may say;
You may name those that are away from court.

FIRST GENTLEMAN.

Your will and pleasure shall be done, my lord.
                    [*Exeunt* Gentlemen.]

VINDICE [*aside*].
"Privately rid forth!"

128. S.P.] *Gentle. Q.*

---

111. *fine*] fine woman (*OED*).
129. *rid forth*] (1) ridden forth; (2) removed by violence (*OED*).

He strives to make sure work on't.                    [*He advances.*]

    —Your good grace!          130

DUKE.

Piato, well done, hast brought her! What lady is't?

VINDICE.

Faith, my lord, a country lady, a little bashful at first, as
most of them are, but after the first kiss, my lord, the worst
is past with them. Your grace knows now what you have to
do. Sh'as somewhat a grave look with her, but—          135

DUKE.

I love that best. Conduct her.

VINDICE [*aside*].                    Have at all.

DUKE.

In gravest looks the greatest faults seem less;
Give me that sin that's rob'd in holiness.

VINDICE [*apart*].

Back with the torch, brother; raise the perfumes.

DUKE.

How sweet can a duke breathe! Age has no fault;          140
Pleasure should meet in a perfumed mist.—
Lady, sweetly encounter'd. I came from court,
I must be bold with you.                    [*He kisses the skull.*]

    O, what's this! O!

VINDICE.

Royal villain! white devil!

DUKE.                    O!

VINDICE.                    Brother,

Place the torch here, that his affrighted eyeballs          145
May start into those hollows. Duke, dost know
Yon dreadful vizard? View it well; 'tis the skull

142–143.] *Collins; prose in* Q.

---

132. *country*] with a glance at the sense in *Hamlet* III.ii.123.

136. *Have at all*] "a desperate risk. A phrase taken from the practice of
gamblers" (Nares); from *have at*, "announcing the speaker's intent to get at
or attack" (*OED*).

140. *fault*] defect.

144. *Royal villain*] seeming oxymoron, of course; cf. I.i.1, note.

144. *white devil*] (1) white-haired devil, (2) hypocrite, the *white devil*
proverbially being worse than the black (Tilley, D 310; cf. D 231 and
2 Cor. 11:14).

Of Gloriana, whom thou poisoned'st last.

DUKE.

    O, 'tas poisoned me.

VINDICE.

    Didst not know that till now?

DUKE.                What are you two?     150

VINDICE.

    Villains, all three!—The very ragged bone
    Has been sufficiently reveng'd.

DUKE.

    O, Hippolito, call treason!

HIPPOLITO.

    Yes, my good lord, treason! treason! treason!

                      *Stamping on him.*

DUKE.

    Then I'm betray'd.                 155

VINDICE.

    Alas, poor lecher, in the hands of knaves:
    A slavish duke is baser than his slaves.

DUKE.

    My teeth are eaten out.

VINDICE.            Hadst any left?

HIPPOLITO.

    I think but few.

VINDICE.

    Then those that did eat are eaten.

DUKE.               O, my tongue!     160

VINDICE.

    Your tongue? 'twill teach you to kiss closer,
    Not like a slobbering Dutchman. You have eyes still:
    Look monster, what a lady hast thou made me
    My once-betrothed wife.

DUKE.            Is it thou, villain?

    Nay, then—

---

162. slobbering] *Hazlitt;* Flobber-    163. me] *Collins;* me, Q.
ing Q.

---

148. *Gloriana*] It is impossible (given the play's imaginatively distanced
English reference) not to recall that this was a favorite name for the idealized
Queen Elizabeth (died 1603).

VINDICE.          'Tis I, 'tis Vindice, 'tis I!                    165
HIPPOLITO.
    And let this comfort thee: our lord and father
    Fell sick upon the infection of thy frowns,
    And died in sadness; be that thy hope of life.
DUKE.
    O!
VINDICE.
    He had his tongue, yet grief made him die speechless.          170
    Pooh! 'tis but early yet; now I'll begin
    To stick thy soul with ulcers. I will make
    Thy spirit grievous sore: it shall not rest,
    But like some pestilent man toss in thy breast.
    Mark me, duke:                                                 175
    Thou'rt a renowned, high, and mighty cuckold.
DUKE.
    O!
VINDICE.
    Thy bastard, thy bastard rides a-hunting in thy brow.
DUKE.
    Millions of deaths!
VINDICE.                    Nay, to afflict thee more,
    Here in this lodge they meet for damned clips;                 180
    Those eyes shall see the incest of their lips.
DUKE.
    Is there a hell besides this, villains?
VINDICE.                                      Villain?
    Nay, heaven is just, scorns are the hires of scorns;
    I ne'er knew yet adulterer without horns.
HIPPOLITO.
    Once ere they die 'tis quitted.        [*Music within.*]
VINDICE.                                Hark, the music;           185
    Their banquet is prepar'd, they're coming—
DUKE.                                                  O
    Kill me not with that sight.

---

180. *clips*] embraces.
183. *scorns*] manifestations of contempt (*OED*).
183. *hires*] (1) recompenses, (2) the actions of hiring.
185. *quitted*] repaid, requited.

VINDICE.                    Thou shalt not lose
    That sight for all thy dukedom.
DUKE.                       Traitors, murderers!
VINDICE.
    What! Is not thy tongue eaten out yet?
    Then we'll invent a silence.—                              190
    Brother, stifle the torch.
DUKE.                       Treason, murder!
VINDICE.
    Nay, faith, we'll have you hush'd. —Now with thy dagger
    Nail down his tongue, and mine shall keep possession
    About his heart; if he but gasp, he dies.
    We dread not death to quittance injuries. Brother,        195
    If he but wink, not brooking the foul object,
    Let our two other hands tear up his lids
    And make his eyes like comets shine through blood:
    When the bad bleeds, then is the tragedy good.
HIPPOLITO.
    Whist, brother! Music's at our ear; they come.            200

            *Enter* [Spurio] *the bastard meeting the* Duchess.

SPURIO.
    Had not that kiss a taste of sin, 'twere sweet.
DUCHESS.
    Why, there's no pleasure sweet, but it is sinful.
SPURIO.
    True; such a bitter sweetness fate hath given,
    Best side to us is the worst side to heaven.
DUCHESS.
    Push, come: 'tis the old duke, thy doubtful father,       205
    The thought of him rubs heaven in thy way.
    But I protest, by yonder waxen fire,
    Forget him, or I'll poison him.
SPURIO.
    Madam, you urge a thought which ne'er had life;

---

195. *quittance*] requite.      196. *brooking*] enduring.
206. *rubs*] "revive, stir up, in respect of memory"; here colored by the intransitive use of the verb in the game of bowls: "to encounter some impediment which retards or diverts [the bowl's] course" (*OED*).

So deadly do I loathe him for my birth,                    210
That if he took me hasp'd within his bed,
I would add murder to adultery,
And with my sword give up his years to death.
DUCHESS.
Why, now thou'rt sociable; let's in and feast:—
Loud'st music sound! Pleasure is banquet's guest.         215
                *Exeunt* [Spurio *and* Duchess].
DUKE.
I cannot brook—                          [Vindice *kills him.*]
VINDICE.                    The brook is turn'd to blood.
HIPPOLITO.
Thanks to loud music.
VINDICE.                    'Twas our friend indeed.
'Tis state in music for a duke to bleed.
The dukedom wants a head, though yet unknown:
As fast as they peep up, let's cut 'em down.          *Exeunt.* 220


[III.vi]    *Enter the Duchess' two sons,* Ambitioso *and* Supervacuo.

AMBITIOSO.
Was not his execution rarely plotted?
We are the duke's sons now.
SUPERVACUO.
Ay, you may thank my policy for that.
AMBITIOSO.
Your policy for what?
SUPERVACUO.
Why, was't not my invention, brother,                      5
To slip the judges? And in lesser compass
Did not I draw the model of his death,

215. banquet's] *Reed;* Banquests *Q.*

---

211. *hasp'd*] a mechanically vivid image for "in the very act of commit-
ting incest."
216. *The brook . . . blood*] Harrier suggests that the "pun may be based
on the metaphor of the King as fountain of honor and life."
[III.vi]
3. *policy*] cf. II.iii.29, note; here, implicitly, "crafty, underhanded
stratagem."
6. *slip*] "elude or evade . . . give the slip to" (*OED*).
7. *model*] design.

Advising you to sudden officers,
And e'en extemporal execution?

AMBITIOSO.

Heart, 'twas a thing I thought on too.                         10

SUPERVACUO.

You thought on't too. 'Sfoot, slander not your thoughts
With glorious untruth; I know 'twas from you.

AMBITIOSO.

Sir, I say, 'twas in my head.

SUPERVACUO.                           Ay, like your brains then,
Ne'er to come out as long as you liv'd.

AMBITIOSO.

You'd have the honor on't, forsooth, that your wit       15
Led him to the scaffold.

SUPERVACUO.                     Since it is my due,
I'll publish't, but I'll ha't in spite of you.

AMBITIOSO.

Methinks y'are much too bold; you should a little
Remember us, brother, next to be honest duke.

SUPERVACUO [aside].

Ay, it shall be as easy for you to be duke              20
As to be honest, and that's never, i'faith.

AMBITIOSO.

Well, cold he is by this time; and because
We're both ambitious, be it our amity,
And let the glory be shar'd equally.

SUPERVACUO.

I am content to that.                                   25

AMBITIOSO.

This night our younger brother shall out of prison;
I have a trick.

SUPERVACUO.       A trick. Prithee, what is't?

AMBITIOSO.

We'll get him out by a wile.

SUPERVACUO.                         Prithee, what wile?

13. S.P. SUPERVACUO] *Reed; Spu. Q.*

---

8. *sudden*] cf. III.iv.20, note.
12. *'twas from you*] i.e., you were incapable of conceiving it.

AMBITIOSO.

No sir, you shall not know it till't be done;
For then you'd swear 'twere yours.                                    30

[*Enter an* Officer, *with a head.*]

SUPERVACUO.

How now, what's he?

AMBITIOSO.                              One of the officers.

SUPERVACUO.

Desired news.

AMBITIOSO.          How now, my friend?

OFFICER.

My lords, under your pardon, I am allotted
To that desertless office, to present you
With the yet bleeding head.

SUPERVACUO [*aside*].                    Ha, ha, excellent.          35

AMBITIOSO [*apart to* Supervacuo].

All's sure our own. Brother, canst weep, think'st thou?
'Twould grace our flattery much. Think of some dame;
'Twill teach thee to dissemble.

SUPERVACUO [*apart to* Ambitioso].   I have thought;
Now for yourself.

AMBITIOSO.                        Our sorrows are so fluent,
Our eyes o'erflow our tongues; words spoke in tears          40
Are like the murmurs of the waters: the sound
Is loudly heard, but cannot be distinguish'd.

SUPERVACUO.

How died he, pray?

OFFICER.                        O, full of rage and spleen.

SUPERVACUO.

He died most valiantly, then; we're glad
To hear it.

OFFICER.          We could not woo him once to pray.          45

AMBITIOSO.

He show'd himself a gentleman in that,
Give him his due.

OFFICER.                      But in the stead of prayer,
He drew forth oaths.

45. woo] *Dodsley;* woe *Q*.          47. stead] *Dodsley;* steed *Q*.

SUPERVACUO.                Then did he pray, dear heart,
Although you understood him not.
OFFICER.                                My lords,
E'en at his last, with pardon be it spoke,                    50
He curs'd you both.
SUPERVACUO.            He curs'd us? 'las, good soul.
AMBITIOSO.
It was not in our powers, but the duke's pleasure.—
[*Aside.*] Finely dissembled o' both sides, sweet fate;
O happy opportunity!

                        *Enter* Lussurioso.

LUSSURIOSO.
Now, my lords—
BOTH.                        O!
LUSSURIOSO.            Why do you shun me, brothers?          55
You may come nearer now;
The savor of the prison has forsook me.
I thank such kind lords as yourselves, I'm free.
AMBITIOSO.
Alive!
SUPERVACUO. In health!
AMBITIOSO.            Releas'd?
We were both e'en amaz'd with joy to see it.                 60
LUSSURIOSO.
I am much to thank you.
SUPERVACUO.
Faith, we spar'd no tongue unto my lord the duke.
AMBITIOSO.
I know your delivery, brother,
Had not been half so sudden but for us.
SUPERVACUO.
O how we pleaded!
LUSSURIOSO.            Most deserving brothers,               65
In my best studies I will think of it.          *Exit* Lussurioso.
AMBITIOSO.
O death and vengeance!
SUPERVACUO.                Hell and torments!
AMBITIOSO.
Slave, cam'st thou to delude us?

OFFICER.                                    Delude you, my lords?
SUPERVACUO.
     Ay, villain; where's this head now?
OFFICER.                                    Why, here, my lord.
     Just after his delivery, you both came                         70
     With warrant from the duke to behead your brother.
AMBITIOSO.
     Ay, our brother, the duke's son.
OFFICER.                                    The duke's son,
     My lord, had his release before you came.
AMBITIOSO.
     Whose head's that then?
OFFICER.                         His whom you left command for,
     Your own brother's.
AMBITIOSO.              Our brother's? O furies!                    75
SUPERVACUO.
     Plagues!
AMBITIOSO.   Confusions!
SUPERVACUO.              Darkness!
AMBITIOSO.                         Devils!
SUPERVACUO.
     Fell it out so accursedly?
AMBITIOSO.                  So damnedly?
SUPERVACUO.
     Villain, I'll brain thee with it.
OFFICER.                              O my good lord!
SUPERVACUO.
     The devil overtake thee!                    [*Exit* Officer.]
AMBITIOSO.                  O fatal.
SUPERVACUO.
     O prodigious to our bloods.
AMBITIOSO.                        Did we dissemble?                 80
SUPERVACUO.
     Did we make our tears women for thee?
AMBITIOSO.
     Laugh and rejoice for thee?
SUPERVACUO.
     Bring warrant for thy death?

81. women] *Dodsley;* woemen *Q.*

AMBITIOSO.                          Mock off thy head?
SUPERVACUO.
You had a trick, you had a wile, forsooth.
AMBITIOSO.
A murrain meet 'em! There's none of these wiles that ever    85
come to good. I see now, there is nothing sure in mortality,
but mortality.
Well, no more words; shalt be reveng'd, i'faith.
Come, throw off clouds now, brother; think of vengeance
And deeper-settled hate. —Sirrah, sit fast,                  90
We'll pull down all, but thou shalt down at last.    *Exeunt.*


[IV.i]            *Enter* Lussurioso *with* Hippolito.

LUSSURIOSO.
Hippolito.
HIPPOLITO.    My lord, has your good lordship
Aught to command me in?
LUSSURIOSO.                       I prithee, leave us.
HIPPOLITO [*aside*].
How's this? come and leave us?
LUSSURIOSO.                       Hippolito.
HIPPOLITO.
Your honor,
I stand ready for any duteous employment.                     5
LUSSURIOSO.
Heart, what mak'st thou here?
HIPPOLITO [*aside*].             A pretty lordly humor:
He bids me to be present to depart; something
Has stung his honor.
LUSSURIOSO.              Be nearer, draw nearer.
Y'are not so good, methinks; I'm angry with you.
HIPPOLITO.
With me, my lord? I'm angry with myself for't.               10

88.] *Hazlitt; prose in* Q.            [IV.i]
                                       9. Y'are] *Collins;* Ye'are Q.

_____

  85. *A . . . 'em*] May a pestilence fall on them.
  90–91. *Sirrah . . . last*] I assume this threat is aimed at the door by which
Lussurioso has left.

LUSSURIOSO.

You did prefer a goodly fellow to me;
'Twas wittily elected, 'twas. I thought
H'ad been a villain, and he proves a knave,
To me a knave.

HIPPOLITO.          I chose him for the best, my lord.

'Tis much my sorrow, if neglect in him                    15
Breed discontent in you.

LUSSURIOSO.          Neglect! 'twas will.

Judge of it:
Firmly to tell of an incredible act,
Not to be thought, less to be spoken of,
'Twixt my stepmother and the bastard, O,                  20
Incestuous sweets between 'em.

HIPPOLITO.          Fie, my lord!

LUSSURIOSO.

I in kind loyalty to my father's forehead
Made this a desperate arm, and in that fury
Committed treason on the lawful bed,
And with my sword e'en rac'd my father's bosom,           25
For which I was within a stroke of death.

HIPPOLITO.

Alack, I'm sorry.—

                    *Enter* Vindice.

                    [*Aside.*] 'Sfoot, just upon the stroke
Jars in my brother; 'twill be villainous music.

VINDICE.

My honored lord.

LUSSURIOSO.          Away!

Prithee forsake us, hereafter we'll not know thee.        30

VINDICE.

Not know me, my lord! Your lordship cannot choose.

LUSSURIOSO.

Begone, I say; thou art a false knave.

23. desperate] *Dodsley;* desperare     27. S.D. *Enter* Vindice] *after* lord.
*Q.*                                      *l. 29 Q.*
                                          31. lordship] *Dodsley;* Lorship *Q.*

16. *will*] i.e., utterly deliberate.     25. *rac'd*] grazed.

VINDICE.

Why, the easier to be known, my lord.

LUSSURIOSO.

Push, I shall prove too bitter with a word,

Make thee a perpetual prisoner,                              35

And lay this iron-age upon thee.

VINDICE [aside].                         Mum,

For there's a doom would make a woman dumb.

Missing the bastard, next him: the wind's come about;

Now 'tis my brother's turn to stay, mine to go out.

                                             *Exit* Vindice.

LUSSURIOSO.

H'as greatly mov'd me.

HIPPOLITO.                   Much to blame, i'faith.         40

LUSSURIOSO.

But I'll recover, to his ruin. 'Twas told me lately, I know

not whether falsely, that you'd a brother.

HIPPOLITO.

Who, I? Yes, my good lord, I have a brother.

LUSSURIOSO.

How chance the court ne'er saw him? Of what nature?

How does he apply his hours?

HIPPOLITO.                        Faith, to curse fates,     45

Who, as he thinks, ordain'd him to be poor:

Keeps at home, full of want and discontent.

LUSSURIOSO [aside].

There's hope in him, for discontent and want

Is the best clay to mold a villain of.—

Hippolito, wish him repair to us;                           50

If there be aught in him to please our blood,

For thy sake we'll advance him, and build fair

His meanest fortunes; for it is in us

To rear up towers from cottages.

38. come] *Dodsley;* comes *Q.*          49. of] *Dodsley;* off *Q.*

---

36. *iron-age*] collection or mass of irons; with play on *Iron Age,* "the last
and worst age of the world according to Greek and Roman mythology,
hence, allusively, an age or period of wickedness, cruelty, oppression,
debasement" (*OED*); cf. V.iii.84.

HIPPOLITO.

    It is so, my lord. He will attend your honor;        55

    But he's a man in whom much melancholy dwells.

LUSSURIOSO.

    Why, the better; bring him to court.

HIPPOLITO.

    With willingness and speed.—

    [*Aside.*] Whom he cast off e'en now, must now succeed.

    Brother, disguise must off;        60

    In thine own shape now I'll prefer thee to him:

    How strangely does himself work to undo him.    *Exit.*

LUSSURIOSO.

    This fellow will come fitly; he shall kill

    That other slave, that did abuse my spleen

    And made it swell to treason. I have put        65

    Much of my heart into him; he must die.

    He that knows great men's secrets, and proves slight,

    That man ne'er lives to see his beard turn white.

    Ay, he shall speed him: I'll employ thee, brother;

    Slaves are but nails to drive out one another.        70

    He being of black condition, suitable

    To want and ill content, hope of preferment

    Will grind him to an edge.

*The* Nobles *enter.*

FIRST NOBLE.

    Good days unto your honor.

LUSSURIOSO.

    My kind lords, I do return the like.        75

SECOND NOBLE.

    Saw you my lord the duke?

LUSSURIOSO.                My lord and father—

    Is he from court?

FIRST NOBLE.         He's sure from court,

71. suitable] *Dodsley;* sutable *Q.*    73.1.] *Dodsley; Q prints in roman type*
                                      *as part of Lussurioso's speech.*

64–65. *abuse . . . swell*] cf. II.iii.5, 27, notes.
67. *slight*] "unworthy of confidence or trust" (*OED*).
71. *of black condition*] melancholic.

But where, which way, his pleasure took we know not,
Nor can we hear on't.

*[Enter the Duke's Gentlemen.]*

LUSSURIOSO.                    Here come those should tell.
Saw you my lord and father?                              80
FIRST GENTLEMAN.
Not since two houres before noon, my lord.
And then he privately rid forth.
LUSSURIOSO.
O, he's rode forth.
FIRST NOBLE.              'Twas wondrous privately.
SECOND NOBLE.
There's none i'th' court had any knowledge on't.
LUSSURIOSO.
His grace is old and sudden; 'tis no treason            85
To say, the duke my father has a humor,
Or such a toy about him; what in us
Would appear light, in him seems virtuous.
FIRST GENTLEMAN.
'Tis oracle, my lord.                              *Exeunt.*


[IV.ii]   *Enter* Vindice *and* Hippolito, Vindice *out of his disguise.*

HIPPOLITO.
So, so, all's as it should be, y'are yourself.
VINDICE.
How that great-villain puts me to my shifts.
HIPPOLITO.
He that did lately in disguise reject thee

81. S.P.] *ascribed to 3. Q.*          89. S.P.] *ascribed to 3. Q.*

---

81. *houres*] disyllabic.
86. *humor*] mere fancy, whim.
87. *toy*] "a foolish or idle fancy; a whim, crotchet, caprice" (*OED*).
88. *light*] frivolous.
[IV.ii]
  2. *that great-villain*] (1) oxymoron, cf. III.v.144, note; (2) arch-villain,
referring to Lussurioso, but with possible secondary reference to the Devil;
cf. l. 9.
  2. *shifts*] (1) fraudulent or evasive devices, stratagems; (2) changes of
clothing (*OED*).

 Shall, now thou art thyself, as much respect thee.

VINDICE.

 'Twill be the quainter fallacy. But brother,     5
 'Sfoot, what use will he put me to now, think'st thou?

HIPPOLITO.

 Nay, you must pardon me in that, I know not.
 H'as some employment for you, but what 'tis
 He and his secretary, the Devil, knows best.

VINDICE.

 Well, I must suit my tongue to his desires,    10
 What color soe'er they be, hoping at last
 To pile up all my wishes on his breast.

HIPPOLITO.

 Faith, brother, he himself shows the way.

VINDICE.

 Now the duke is dead, the realm is clad in clay.
 His death being not yet known, under his name   15
 The people still are govern'd. Well, thou his son
 Art not long-liv'd; thou shalt not joy his death.
 To kill thee, then, I should most honor thee;
 For 'twould stand firm in every man's belief,
 Thou'st a kind child, and only died'st with grief.  20

HIPPOLITO.

 You fetch about well, but let's talk in present.
 How will you appear in fashion different,
 As well as in apparel, to make all things possible?
 If you be but once tripp'd, we fall forever.

---

 5. *quainter*] more ingeniously elaborated, elegantly refined.
 9. *secretary*] in the root sense, "one who is entrusted with private or secret matters" (*OED*).
 12. *To . . . breast*] The image is drawn from pressing to death with weights.
 14. *clad in clay*] Some editors have supposed the text corrupt here, and it may be. But the rather obscure figure appears to rest on two commonplaces: the flesh as "clothing" (cf. I.i.31), and the identity of the ruler with the realm and body politic. The phrase occurs, in a simpler sense, in Spenser, *The Shepheardes Calender*, "October," l. 61: "But ah! Mecoenas is yclad in claye."
 16. *thou*] i.e., Lussurioso.
 21. *fetch about*] "take a round about course or method" (*OED*).
 24. *tripp'd . . . forever*] The spiritual sense is dramatically pertinent.

It is not the least policy to be doubtful;                    25
You must change tongue—familiar was your first.

VINDICE.

Why, I'll bear me in some strain of melancholy,
And string myself with heavy-sounding wire,
Like such an instrument
That speaks merry things sadly.

HIPPOLITO.                              Then 'tis as I meant;    30
I gave you out at first in discontent.

VINDICE.

I'll turn myself, and then—

*[Enter Lussurioso.]*

HIPPOLITO.                              'Sfoot, here he comes;
Hast thought upon't?

VINDICE.                          Salute him, fear not me.

LUSSURIOSO.

Hippolito.

HIPPOLITO.          Your lordship.

LUSSURIOSO.                         What's he yonder?

HIPPOLITO.                                                    35
'Tis Vindice, my discontented brother,
Whom, 'cording to your will, I've brought to court.

LUSSURIOSO.

Is that thy brother? Beshrew me, a good presence.
I wonder h'as been from the court so long.—
Come nearer.

HIPPOLITO.

Brother, Lord Lussurioso, the duke's son.              40

36. I've] *Dodsley;* I'ave *Q*.          40. duke's] *Dodsley;* Duke *Q*.

---

25. *doubtful*] apprehensive (and therefore precautious).

26. *familiar*] The adjectival sense of course is "unceremonious, taking liberties"; but there is a glance at the substantive in the sense, "a demon supposed to be in association with or under the power of a man" (*OED*).

27. *strain*] (1) kind; and playing on the musical sense, (2) melody, tune.

32. *turn*] (1) change, transmute; (2) "move circularly, as on a pivot . . . so as ultimately to face in the opposite direction" (*OED*); (3) in a musical sense, as in tuning a string instrument.

33. *fear not me*] don't worry about me.

LUSSURIOSO.

Be more near to us; welcome; nearer yet.

[Vindice] *snatches off his hat and makes legs to him.*

VINDICE.

How don you? God you good den.

LUSSURIOSO.                    We thank thee.

How strangely such a course-homely salute
Shows in the palace, where we greet in fire,
Nimble and desperate tongues. Should we name      45
God in a salutation, 'twould ne'er be stood on—heaven!
Tell me, what has made thee so melancholy?

VINDICE.

Why, going to law.

LUSSURIOSO.

Why, will that make a man melancholy?

VINDICE.

Yes, to look long upon ink and black buckram. I went me to    50
law in *Anno quadragesimo secundo*, and I waded out of it in
*Anno sextagesimo tertio*.

LUSSURIOSO.

What, three and twenty years in law?

VINDICE.

I have known those that have been five and fifty, and all
about pullen and pigs.                                   55

LUSSURIOSO.

May it be possible such men should breathe,
To vex the terms so much?

VINDICE.                 'Tis food to some, my lord.
There are old men at the present, that are so poisoned with
the affectation of law-words (having had many suits can-

---

41.1] *Q prints in margin beside ll.*    42. good] *Hazlitt;* god *Q*.
40–42.                          46. on] *Hazlitt;* on't *Q*.

---

42. *God . . . den*] God give you good even.
45. *tongues*] disyllabic.
46. *stood on*] here (apparently), "accepted, tolerated."
50. *black buckram*] an attorney's bag.
51. *Anno . . . secundo*] the forty-second year (of the reign).
52. *Anno . . . tertio*] the sixty-third year.      55. *pullen*] poultry.
57. *terms*] the times during which court is in session.

vass'd), that their common talk is nothing but Barbary    60
Latin. They cannot so much as pray but in law, that their
sins may be remov'd with a writ of error, and their souls
fetch'd up to heaven with a sasarara.

LUSSURIOSO.

It seems most strange to me;
Yet all the world meets round in the same bent:              65
Where the heart's set, there goes the tongue's consent.
How dost apply thy studies, fellow?

VINDICE.                              Study?
Why, to think how a great rich man lies a-dying, and a
poor cobbler tolls the bell for him. How he cannot depart
the world and see the great chest stand before him; when   70
he lies speechless, how he will point you readily to all the
boxes; and when he is past all memory, as the gossips guess,
then thinks he of forfeitures and obligations; nay, when
to all men's hearings he whurls and rottles in the throat,

64. S.P.] *Gilchrist conj.; speech as-*
*signed to Hippolito Q.*

---

60–61. *Barbary Latin*] barbarous Latin.
62. *writ of error*] "a writ brought to procure the reverse of a judgement,
on the ground of error" (*OED*).
63. *sasarara*] corruption of *certiorari*, the name of "a writ issuing from a
superior court, upon the complaint of a party that he has not received
justice in an inferior court or cannot have an impartial trial, by which the
records of the cause are called up for trial in the superior court" (*OED*).
66. *there . . . consent*] i.e., the tongue agrees in action. The expression
assumes the physiological notion of a "sympathy between one organ or part
of the body and another, whereby when the one is affected, the other is
affected correspondingly" (*OED*).
73. *forfeitures and obligations*] These terms are selected for their ironic as
well as their literal appropriateness.
73. *forfeitures*] "the fact of losing or becoming liable to deprivation of
(an estate, goods, life, an office, right, etc.) in consequence of a crime,
offence, or breach of engagement"; "that which is forfeited" (*OED*).
73. *obligations*] "An agreement, enforceable by law, whereby a person
or persons become bound to the payment of a sum of money, or other
performance; the document containing such an agreement; esp[ecially] in
Eng[lish] Law, a written contract or bond under seal containing a penalty
with a condition annexed. Also, the right created or liability incurred by
such an agreement" (*OED*).
74. *whurls and rottles*] onomatopoeic words descriptive of rattling in the
throat.

he's busy threat'ning his poor tenants. And this would    75
last me now some seven years' thinking or thereabouts. But,
I have a conceit a-coming in picture upon this. I draw it
myself, which i'faith, la, I'll present to your honor; you shall
not choose but like it, for your lordship shall give me
nothing for it.                                           80

LUSSURIOSO.
Nay, you mistake me then,
For I am publish'd bountiful enough.
Let's taste of your conceit.

VINDICE.                    In picture, my lord?

LUSSURIOSO.
Ay, in picture.

VINDICE.            Marry, this it is—
*A usuring father, to be boiling in hell, and his son and heir with*    85
*a whore dancing over him.*

HIPPOLITO [*aside*].
H'as par'd him to the quick.

LUSSURIOSO.
The conceit's pretty, i'faith,
But take't upon my life, 'twill ne'er be lik'd.

VINDICE.
No? why I'm sure the whore will be lik'd well enough.    90

HIPPOLITO [*aside*].
Ay, if she were out o'th' picture, he'd like her then himself.

VINDICE.
And as for the son and heir, he shall be an eyesore to no
young revelers, for he shall be drawn in cloth of gold
breeches.

LUSSURIOSO.
And thou hast put my meaning in the pockets,            95
And canst not draw that out? My thought was this:
To see the picture of a usuring father
Boiling in hell, our rich men would ne'er like it.

79. choose] *Dodsley* (chuse); chose     95. pockets] *Dodsley;* pock (ets
*Q.*                                      *dropped to end of next line*) *Q.*

77. *conceit*] (1) artistic conception, (2) witty figure.
77. *in picture*] i.e., an emblematic one.
82. *publish'd*] reported.

VINDICE.

    O true, I cry you heartily mercy. I know the reason, for some
    of 'em had rather be damn'd indeed than damn'd in colors.  100

LUSSURIOSO [aside].

    A parlous melancholy! H'as wit enough
    To murder any man, and I'll give him means.—
    I think thou art ill-monied?

VINDICE.               Money! ho, ho.

    'Tas been my want so long, 'tis now my scoff;
    I've e'en forgot what color silver's of.         105

LUSSURIOSO [aside].

    It hits as I could wish.

VINDICE.          I get good clothes

    Of those that dread my humor, and for table-room
    I feed on those that cannot be rid of me.

LUSSURIOSO.

    Somewhat to set thee up withal.      [He gives him gold.]

VINDICE.

    O, mine eyes!

LUSSURIOSO.      How now, man?

VINDICE.             Almost struck blind;    110

    This bright unusual shine to me seems proud;
    I dare not look till the sun be in a cloud.

LUSSURIOSO [aside].

    I think I shall affect his melancholy.—
    How are they now?

VINDICE.         The better for your asking.

LUSSURIOSO.

    You shall be better yet if you but fasten      115
    Truly on my intent. Now y'are both present,
    I will unbrace such a close private villain

---

105. of] Dodsley; off Q.        106. clothes] Hazlitt; cloths Q.

---

    99. I . . . mercy] I heartily beg your pardon.
    100. damn'd in colors] condemned in a (mere) painted picture.
    101. parlous] dangerously cunning, keen, capable of harming (OED).
    111. proud] magnificent, splendid.    113. affect] like.
    117. unbrace] in the figurative sense, "disclose"; here ironic because the
literal sense, "undress," reminds us he really is referring to a "shape," a
costume used for disguise.

Unto your vengeful swords, the like ne'er heard of,
Who hath disgrac'd you much and injur'd us.

HIPPOLITO.
Disgraced us, my lord?

LUSSURIOSO.                    Ay, Hippolito.                    120
I kept it here till now, that both your angers
Might meet him at once.

VINDICE.                    I'm covetous
To know the villain.

LUSSURIOSO [to Hippolito].   You know him, that slave pander
Piato, whom we threatened last
With irons in perpetual 'prisonment.                    125

VINDICE [aside].
All this is I.

HIPPOLITO.        Is't he, my lord?

LUSSURIOSO.                    I'll tell you;
You first prefer'd him to me.

VINDICE.                    Did you, brother?

HIPPOLITO.
I did indeed.

LUSSURIOSO.        And the ingrateful villain,
To quit that kindness, strongly wrought with me,
Being as you see a likely man for pleasure,                    130
With jewels to corrupt your virgin sister.

HIPPOLITO.
O villain!

VINDICE.        He shall surely die that did it.

LUSSURIOSO.
I, far from thinking any virgin harm,
Especially knowing her to be as chaste
As that part which scarce suffers to be touch'd,                    135
Th' eye, would not endure him.

VINDICE.                    Would you not, my lord;
'Twas wondrous honorably done.

LUSSURIOSO.
But with some fine frowns kept him out.

138. fine] *Collins;* fiue *Q.*

---

121. *here*] i.e., within my breast, to myself (with gesture).
122. *meet*] apart from the obvious meaning, also in the sense, "to be
even with, requite, pay out" (*OED*).

VINDICE.                          Out, slave!

LUSSURIOSO.

    What did me he but, in revenge of that,
    Went of his own free will to make infirm                    140
    Your sister's honor, whom I honor with my soul
    For chaste respect; and not prevailing there
    (As 'twas but desperate folly to attempt it),
    In mere spleen, by the way, waylays your mother,
    Whose honor being a coward, as it seems,                    145
    Yielded by little force.

VINDICE.                    Coward indeed.

LUSSURIOSO.

    He, proud of their advantage, (as he thought)
    Brought me these news for happy; but I, heaven
    Forgive me for't—

VINDICE.                    What did your honor?

LUSSURIOSO.

    —In rage push'd him from me,                               150
    Trampled beneath his throat, spurn'd him, and bruis'd:
    Indeed I was too cruel, to say troth.

HIPPOLITO.

    Most nobly manag'd!

VINDICE [aside].

    Has not heaven an ear? Is all the lightning wasted?

LUSSURIOSO.

    If I now were so impatient in a modest cause,              155
    What should you be?

VINDICE.                    Full mad; he shall not live
    To see the moon change.

LUSSURIOSO.                    He's about the palace.
    Hippolito, entice him this way, that thy brother
    May take full mark of him.

HIPPOLITO.

    Heart! that shall not need, my lord;                       160
    I can direct him so far.

---

144. *spleen*] here: impulse, caprice.
147. *their advantage*] *their* refers (I think) to *these news* (l. 148), the involuted
structure serving (as frequently) to expose dramatically the calculation of the
lie. The word *advantage* thus denotes the "favoring circumstance . . . which
gives the superiority" (*OED*).

LUSSURIOSO.             Yet for my hate's sake,
     Go, wind him this way; I'll see him bleed myself.
HIPPOLITO [*apart to* Vindice].
     What now, brother?
VINDICE [*apart to* Hippolito].
     Nay, e'en what you will; y'are put to it, brother!
HIPPOLITO [*aside*].
     An impossible task, I'll swear,            165
     To bring him hither that's already here.     *Exit* Hippolito.
LUSSURIOSO.
     Thy name? I have forgot it.
VINDICE.                  Vindice, my lord.
LUSSURIOSO.
     'Tis a good name that.
VINDICE.                  Ay, a revenger.
LUSSURIOSO.
     It does betoken courage; thou shouldst be valiant,
     And kill thine enemies.
VINDICE.            That's my hope, my lord.       170
LUSSURIOSO.
     This slave is one.
VINDICE.         I'll doom him.
LUSSURIOSO.             Then I'll praise thee!
     Do thou observe me best, and I'll best raise thee.

                 [*Re-*]*enter* Hippolito.

VINDICE.
     Indeed, I thank you.
LUSSURIOSO.
     Now, Hippolito, where's the slave pander?
HIPPOLITO.
     Your good lordship would have            175
     A loathsome sight of him, much offensive.
     He's not in case now to be seen, my lord;

---

162. *wind*] "turn or deflect in a certain direction" (*OED*), the ensuing
*bleed* supporting Harrier's reading as a hunting metaphor: "'drive him down
wind by letting him scent you.'"
    164. *y'are . . . it*] you are "forced to do your utmost" (*OED*).
    172. *observe*] show respectful attention to; humor, gratify (*OED*).

The worst of all the deadly sins is in him,
That beggarly damnation, drunkenness.

LUSSURIOSO.
Then he's a double slave.

VINDICE [aside].                    'Twas well convey'd,                    180
Upon a sudden wit.

LUSSURIOSO.                    What, are you both
Firmly resolv'd? I'll see him dead myself.

VINDICE.
Or else, let not us live.

LUSSURIOSO.                    You may direct
Your brother to take note of him.

HIPPOLITO.                    I shall.

LUSSURIOSO.
Rise but in this, and you shall never fall.                    185

VINDICE.
Your honor's vassals.

LUSSURIOSO [aside].                    This was wisely carried.
Deep policy in us makes fools of such:
Then must a slave die when he knows too much.

                                        *Exit* Lussurioso.

VINDICE.
O, thou almighty patience! 'Tis my wonder
That such a fellow, impudent and wicked,                    190
Should not be cloven as he stood,
Or with a secret wind burst open!
Is there no thunder left, or is't kept up
In stock for heavier vengeance? [*Thunder.*] There it goes!

HIPPOLITO.
Brother, we lose ourselves.

---

178. *worst . . . sins*] "emphasizing the play's strong view of drink"
(Harrier).
180. *convey'd*] managed.
194. S.D. *Thunder*] an instance of Elizabethan symbolic representation
difficult for modern readers (to whom the abrupt literalization of the
figurative thunder is apt to appear ludicrous). The method economically
affords emphasis on the objective presence of "that eternal eye/ That sees
through flesh and all" (I.iii.66–67), and on its impending judgments,
essential to the play's complexly ironic interplays and contrasts of earthly
and divine justice and vengeance; cf. V.iii.0.3, 41.2.

VINDICE.                    But I have found it.          195
'Twill hold, 'tis sure; thanks, thanks to any spirit
That mingled it 'mongst my inventions.

HIPPOLITO.
What is't?

VINDICE.          'Tis sound, and good; thou shalt partake it.
I'm hir'd to kill myself.

HIPPOLITO.                    True.

VINDICE.                    Prithee, mark it.
And the old duke being dead, but not convey'd,          200
For he's already miss'd too, and you know
Murder will peep out of the closest husk—

HIPPOLITO.
Most true.

VINDICE.          What say you then to this device?
If we dress'd up the body of the duke—

HIPPOLITO.
In that disguise of yours.

VINDICE.                    Y'are quick, y'ave reach'd it.          205

HIPPOLITO.
I like it wonderously.

VINDICE.
And being in drink, as you have publish'd him,
To lean him on his elbow, as if sleep had caught him,
Which claims most interest in such sluggy men.

HIPPOLITO.
Good yet, but here's a doubt:          210
We, thought by th' duke's son to kill that pander,
Shall, when he is known, be thought to kill the duke.

VINDICE.
Neither—O thanks—it is substantial:

211. We,] *Dodsley;* Me *Q.*

---

200. *convey'd*] taken away, removed; with the additional senses, "trans-
ferred or made over (as property) to another," "brought down by succes-
sion" (*OED*), possibly required by an implicit shift of subject (from *the old
duke* to his title), impelled by the thought that his body will be discovered.
203. *device*] stratagem, plot.
209. *sluggy*] sluggish.
213. *substantial*] firmly based, of unchanging nature, and thus of solid
worth.

For that disguise being on him which I wore, it will be
thought I, which he calls the pander, did kill the duke and   215
fled away in his apparel, leaving him so disguis'd to avoid
swift pursuit.

HIPPOLITO.
Firmer and firmer.

VINDICE.                    Nay, doubt not 'tis in grain;
I warrant it hold color.

HIPPOLITO.                  Let's about it.

VINDICE.
But by the way too, now I think on't, brother,              220
Let's conjure that base devil out of our mother.        *Exeunt.*


[IV.iii]

*Enter the Duchess arm in arm with [Spurio] the Bastard; he seemeth
lasciviously to her. After them, enter Supervacuo, running with a rapier;
his brother [Ambitioso] stops him.*

SPURIO.
Madam, unlock yourself; should it be seen,
Your arm would be suspected.

DUCHESS.
Who is't that dares suspect or this or these?
May not we deal our favors where we please?

SPURIO.
I'm confident you may.        *Exeunt [Spurio and* Duchess].

AMBITIOSO.                  'Sfoot, brother, hold.              5

SUPERVACUO.
Would't let the bastard shame us?

AMBITIOSO.                      Hold, hold, brother!
There's fitter time than now.

SUPERVACUO.                  Now, when I see it.

AMBITIOSO.
'Tis too much seen already.

SUPERVACUO.                  Seen and known.
The nobler she's, the baser is she grown.

---

0.1 *seemeth*] acts.
1. *unlock yourself*] i.e., separate (from me).
3. *or . . . these*] either this or these (gestures of affection).

AMBITIOSO.

    If she were bent lasciviously, the fault               10

    Of mighty women that sleep soft—O death!

    Must she needs choose such an unequal sinner,

    To make all worse?

SUPERVACUO.           A bastard, the duke's bastard!

    Shame heap'd on shame.

AMBITIOSO.           O our disgrace!

    Most women have small waist the world throughout;    15

    But their desires are thousand miles about.

SUPERVACUO.

    Come, stay not here, let's after and prevent;

    Or else they'll sin faster than we'll repent.        *Exeunt.*

## [IV.iv]

*Enter* Vindice *and* Hippolito *bringing out* [Gratiana,] *their mother, one by one shoulder, and the other by the other, with daggers in their hands.*

VINDICE.

    O thou! for whom no name is bad enough.

GRATIANA.

    What means my sons? what, will you murder me?

VINDICE.

    Wicked, unnatural parent.

HIPPOLITO.           Fiend of women.

GRATIANA.

    O! are sons turn'd monsters? Help!

VINDICE.           In vain.

GRATIANA.

    Are you so barbarous to set iron nipples           5

    Upon the breast that gave you suck?

VINDICE.           That breast

    Is turn'd to quarled poison.

15. waist] waste *Q.*
16. their] *Dodsley;* there *Q.*
17–18.] *Q corr.; Q uncorr. prints in reverse order, with l. 18 as last line of Ambitioso's speech.*

18. S.D.] *Dodsley; after l.16 Q corr.; after* repent *Q uncorr.*
[IV.iv]
0.1 *their] Dodsley;* there *Q.*
3. parent] *Dodsley;* Parents *Q.*

7. *quarled*] This appears to mean "curdled."

GRATIANA.

Cut not your days for't; am not I your mother?

VINDICE.

Thou dost usurp that title now by fraud,
For in that shell of mother breeds a bawd.                    10

GRATIANA.

A bawd? O name far loathsomer than hell.

HIPPOLITO.

It should be so, knew'st thou thy office well.

GRATIANA.

I hate it.

VINDICE.

Ah, is't possible, Thou only God on high,
That women should dissemble when they die?                    15

GRATIANA.

Dissemble?

VINDICE.          Did not the duke's son direct
A fellow of the world's condition hither,
That did corrupt all that was good in thee?
Made thee uncivilly forget thyself,
And work our sister to his lust?

GRATIANA.                    Who, I?                    20
That had been monstrous! I defy that man
For any such intent. None lives so pure,
But shall be soil'd with slander.
Good son, believe it not.

VINDICE [aside].          O I'm in doubt
Whether I'm myself or no!—                    25
Stay, let me look again upon this face.
Who shall be sav'd when mothers have no grace?

HIPPOLITO.

'Twould make one half despair.

VINDICE.                    I was the man.
Defy me now; let's see, do't modestly.

GRATIANA.

O hell unto my soul.                    30

---

12. knew'st] knewst Q corr.; knowst          14. Thou only God] Swinburne conj.;
Q uncorr.                    Thou onely, you powers Q.

---

8. Cut . . . mother] cf. II.ii.95–96, note.

VINDICE.

    In that disguise, I, sent from the duke's son,

    Tried you, and found you base metal,

    As any villain might have done.

GRATIANA.                              O no,

    No tongue but yours could have bewitch'd me so.

VINDICE.

    O nimble in damnation, quick in tune.                    35

    There is no devil could strike fire so soon:

    I am confuted in a word.

GRATIANA.

    O sons, forgive me! To myself I'll prove more true;

    You that should honor me, I kneel to you.

                            [*She kneels and weeps.*]

VINDICE.

    A mother to give aim to her own daughter!                40

HIPPOLITO.

    True, brother; how far beyond nature 'tis,

    Though many mothers do't.

VINDICE.

    Nay, and you draw tears once, go you to bed.—

    Wet will make iron blush and change to red:

    Brother, it rains; 'twill spoil your dagger; house it.     45

HIPPOLITO.

    'Tis done.

VINDICE.

    I'faith, 'tis a sweet shower, it does much good;

    The fruitful grounds and meadows of her soul

41. 'tis] *Q corr., state 3;* to't *Q uncorr.* (*states 1 and 2*).     44. Wet] *Q corr., state 2;* Wee *Q uncorr.* (*state 1*).

43. tears] teares *Q state 1 and corr., state 3;* tares *Q* (*erroneously*) *corr., state 2.*     44. iron] yron *Q corr., state 3;* you *Q uncorr.* (*states 1 and 2*).

---

32. *Tried . . . metal*] cf. I.iii.182, note.

36. *There . . . soon*] i.e., as myself.

40. *give aim to*] to guide another's aim by telling him the results of a previous shot; thus, here, "direct, incite."

48–49. *fruitful . . . dry*] This traditional imagery of spiritual "dryness," "sterility," and "fruitfulness" in virtues and good works (based, ultimately, on Genesis 1:28) enjoys a peculiar intensity in the present poetic context because of the playwright's virtual identification of stable moral and social values with the landed order of the old-fashioned manor.

Has been long dry. Pour down, thou blessed dew.—
Rise, mother; troth, this shower has made you higher.    50
GRATIANA.

O you heavens!
Take this infectious spot out of my soul.
I'll rinse it in seven waters of mine eyes!
Make my tears salt enough to taste of grace:
To weep is to our sex naturally given;    55
But to weep truly, that's a gift from heaven.
VINDICE.

Nay, I'll kiss you now. —Kiss her, brother.
Let's marry her to our souls, wherein's no lust,
And honorably love her.
HIPPOLITO.                    Let it be.
VINDICE.

For honest women are so seld and rare,    60
'Tis good to cherish those poor few that are.—
O you of easy wax, do but imagine,
Now the disease has left you, how leprously
That office would have cling'd unto your forehead.
All mothers that had any graceful hue    65
Would have worn masks to hide their face at you.
It would have grown to this: at your foul name,
Green-color'd maids would have turn'd red with shame.
HIPPOLITO.

And then our sister, full of hire, and baseness.
VINDICE.

There had been boiling lead again.    70

64. cling'd] *Q corr., state 3;* cling
*Q uncorr. (states 1 and 2).*

---

51–56. *O . . . heaven*] based on the Protestant doctrinal emphasis on the
inseparability of "true" repentance from faith: "For by grace are ye saved
through faith; and that not of yourselves: It is the gift of God" (Ephesians
2:8).
54. *salt*] Apart from the obvious reference to the salinity of tears, there
is likely allusion to salt in the symbolic sense in which it is used in baptism,
as a sign that the person being baptized "should be delivered from the
corruption of sin" (Catechism of the Council of Trent).
60. *seld*] infrequent.        65. *hue*] (1) kind, (2) complexion.
68. *Green-color'd*] unripe, immature, inexperienced.
69. *hire*] payment for temporary use; with a bitter pun (as the ensuing
*baseness* shows) on "higher."

The duke's son's great concubine!
A drab of state, a cloth o' silver slut,
To have her train borne up, and her soul trail i'th' dirt.
Great—
HIPPOLITO.   To be miserably great, rich, to be
Eternally wretched.
VINDICE.                O common madness.                    75
Ask but the thriving'st harlot in cold blood,
She'd give the world to make her honor good.
Perhaps you'll say, but only to th' duke's son,
In private. Why, she first begins with one,
Who afterward to thousand proves a whore:          80
"Break ice in one place, it will crack in more."
GRATIANA.
Most certainly applied.
HIPPOLITO.
O brother, you forget our business.
VINDICE.
And well remember'd. Joy's a subtle elf;
I think man's happiest when he forgets himself.—    85
Farewell, once dried, now holy-water'd mead;
Our hearts wear feathers that before wore lead.
GRATIANA.
I'll give you this: that one I never knew
Flead better for, and 'gainst the devil, than you.
VINDICE.
You make me proud on't.                              90
HIPPOLITO.
Commend us in all virtue to our sister.

71. The duke's] The dukes *Q corr.*,    74. To be] *Q corr., state 3;* Too *Q*
*state 3;* Dukes *Q uncorr. (states 1 and    uncorr. (states 1 and 2).*
2).*

71. *duke's*] disyllabic; cf. I.i.28, note.
   86. *holy-water'd*] figuratively asserting that her tears represented spiritually
genuine contrition and repentance, indeed were *salt enough to taste of grace*
(l. 54). The image recalls and poetically realizes ll. 48–50, and depends upon
the fact that salt is "exorcised and blessed in the preparation of holy water
for the Asperges before High Mass on Sunday and for the use of the faithful
in their homes" (*The Catholic Encyclopoedia*).
   90. *on't*] of it.

VINDICE.

Ay, for the love of heaven, to that true maid.

GRATIANA.

With my best words.

VINDICE. Why, that was motherly said.

*Exeunt* [Vindice *and* Hippolito].

GRATIANA.

I wonder now what fury did transport me?
I feel good thoughts begin to settle in me. 95
O, with what forehead can I look on her,
Whose honor I've so impiously beset?

[*Enter* Castiza.]

And here she comes.

CASTIZA.

Now, mother, you have wrought with me so strongly,
That what for my advancement, as to calm 100
The trouble of your tongue, I am content.

GRATIANA.

Content to what?

CASTIZA. To do as you have wish'd me,
To prostitute my breast to the duke's son,
And put myself to common usury.

GRATIANA.

I hope you will not so.

CASTIZA. Hope you I will not? 105
That's not the hope you look to be saved in.

GRATIANA.

Truth, but it is.

CASTIZA. Do not deceive yourself;

---

100. *as*] so as.

103. *duke's*] disyllabic, cf. I.i.28, note.

104. *common*] (1) in the sense used "of criminals, offenders, and offences" (with the implications, "public, apert, overt, confessed, the subject of common report, notorious, habitual"); (2) existing for the use of the public; (3) ordinary (*OED*).

104. *usury*] use for hire, prostitution; the figurative use of the term (cf. *Measure for Measure* III.ii.7) permits the playwright to fuse his symbolic sense of sexual corruption and his hatred of a money economy.

106. *hope . . . in*] alluding sourly to Gratiana's commercial perversion of "For we are saved by hope" (Romans 8:24).

I am, as you e'en out of marble wrought.
What would you now? Are ye not pleas'd yet with me?
You shall not wish me to be more lascivious          110
Than I intend to be.

GRATIANA.                    Strike not me cold.

CASTIZA.
How often have you charg'd me on your blessing
To be a cursed woman? When you knew
Your blessing had no force to make me lewd,
You laid your curse upon me; that did more.          115
The mother's curse is heavy: where that fights,
Sons set in storm, and daughters lose their lights.

GRATIANA.
Good child, dear maid, if there be any spark
Of heavenly intellectual fire within thee,
O let my breath revive it to a flame!          120
Put not all out with woman's wilful follies.
I am recover'd of that foul disease
That haunts too many mothers; kind, forgive me,
Make me not sick in health. If then
My words prevail'd when they were wickedness,          125
How much more now when they are just and good?

CASTIZA.
I wonder what you mean? Are not you she
For whose infect persuasions I could scarce
Kneel out my prayers, and had much ado,
In three hours' reading, to untwist so much          130
Of the black serpent as you wound about me?

GRATIANA.
'Tis unfruitful, held tedious, to repeat what's past.
I'm now your present mother.

CASTIZA.                    Push, now 'tis too late.

GRATIANA.
Bethink again, thou know'st not what thou say'st.

---

108. *out of marble*] i.e., permanently, with additional reference to impudence (cf. V.iii.68). (The pointing is that of Q.)
123. *kind*] primarily as vocative for "child," the emphasis being on the
attempted reestablishment of natural relationships and values; also in the
usual sense of the word.

CASTIZA.

No?—"Deny advancement, treasure, the duke's son!"        135
GRATIANA.

O see, I spoke those words, and now they poison me.
What will the deed do then?
Advancement?—True: as high as shame can pitch.
For treasure—who e'er knew a harlot rich?
Or could build by the purchase of her sin                    140
An hospital to keep their bastards in?
The duke's son?—O, when women are young
Courtiers, they are sure to be old beggars.
To know the miseries most harlots taste,
Thou'dst wish thyself unborn, when thou art unchaste.      145
CASTIZA.

O mother, let me twine about your neck,
And kiss you till my soul melt on your lips.
I did but this to try you.
GRATIANA.                      O speak truth!
CASTIZA.

Indeed, I did not; for no tongue has force to alter me from
honest.                                                       150
If maidens would, men's words could have no power;
A virgin honor is a crystal tower,
Which, being weak, is guarded with good spirits;
Until she basely yields, no ill inherits.
GRATIANA.

O happy child! Faith and thy birth hath saved me.            155
'Mongst thousand daughters, happiest of all others,
Be thou a glass for maids, and I for mothers.      *Exeunt.*

157. Be] *Reed;* Buy *Q.*

---

135. *duke's*] disyllabic; cf. I.i.28, note.
149. *did not*] i.e., did not speak truth when I said I was ready to prostitute
myself.
152. *crystal*] cf. II.i.240.
157. *glass*] the figurative looking-glass; i.e., a model.

[V.i]

*Enter* Vindice *and* Hippolito [*with the Duke's corpse dressed in Vindice's Piato disguise; they set it in place*].

VINDICE.
So, so, he leans well; take heed you wake him not,
Brother.

HIPPOLITO. I warrant you, my life for yours.

VINDICE.
That's a good lay, for I must kill myself.
Brother, that's I, that sits for me; do you mark it. And I
must stand ready here to make away my self yonder. I must 5
sit to be kill'd, and stand to kill myself. I could vary it not
so little as thrice over again; 'tas some eight returns, like
Michaelmas Term.

HIPPOLITO.
That's enow, o' conscience.

VINDICE.
But, sirrah, does the duke's son come single? 10

HIPPOLITO.
No, there's the hell on't. His faith's too feeble to go alone;
he brings flesh-flies after him that will buzz against supper-
time, and hum for his coming out.

VINDICE.
Ah, the fly-flop of vengeance beat 'em to pieces! Here was
the sweetest occasion, the fittest hour, to have made my 15
revenge familiar with him: show him the body of the duke
his father, and how quaintly he died like a politician, in
hugger-mugger, made no man acquainted with it; and in
catastrophe, slain him over his father's breast, and—O, I'm
mad to lose such a sweet opportunity. 20

HIPPOLITO.
Nay, push, prithee be content. There's no remedy present.

11. faith's] *Q corr.;* faith *Q uncorr.*    17. died] *Q corr.;* did *Q uncorr.*

3. *lay*] wager.
7. *returns*] playing on the legal term for the sheriff's reports to the court
on the action taken on the writs issued from it.
9. *enow*] enough.
14. *fly-flop*] "an instrument for driving away flies" (*OED*).
17. *quaintly*] ingeniously, cunningly.   17–18. *in hugger-mugger*] in secret.

May not hereafter times open in as fair faces as this?

VINDICE.

They may, if they can paint so well.

HIPPOLITO.

Come, now to avoid all suspicion, let's forsake this room,
and be going to meet the duke's son.                              25

VINDICE.

Content, I'm for any weather. Heart, step close; here he
comes.

*Enter* Lussurioso.

HIPPOLITO.

My honor'd lord.

LUSSURIOSO.                    O me! you both present?

VINDICE.

E'en newly, my lord, just as your lordship enter'd now.
About this place we had notice given he should be, but in    30
some loathsome plight or other.

HIPPOLITO.

Came your honor private?

LUSSURIOSO.

Private enough for this; only a few
Attend my coming out.

VINDICE [*aside*].            Death rot those few.

LUSSURIOSO.

Stay, yonder's the slave.                                        35

VINDICE.

Mass, there's the slave indeed, my lord.—
[*Aside.*] 'Tis a good child; he calls his father slave.

LUSSURIOSO.

Ay, that's the villain, the damn'd villain. Softly,
Tread easy.

VINDICE.            Pooh, I warrant you, my lord;
We'll stifle in our breaths.

LUSSURIOSO.                    That will do well.—              40
Base rogue, thou sleepest thy last.— [*Aside.*] 'Tis policy
To have him kill'd in's sleep, for if he wak'd
He would betray all to them.

31. loathsome] *Q corr.;* leathsome
*Q uncorr.*

VINDICE.                          But, my lord—

LUSSURIOSO.

    Ha, what say'st?

VINDICE.                Shall we kill him now he's drunk?

LUSSURIOSO.

    Ay, best of all.

VINDICE.              Why then he will ne'er live                    45

    To be sober.

LUSSURIOSO.          No matter, let him reel to hell.

VINDICE.

    But being so full of liquor, I fear he will

    Put out all the fire—

LUSSURIOSO.                    Thou art a mad beast.

VINDICE [aside].

    —And leave none to warm your lordship's golls withal.—

    [Aloud.]   For he that dies drunk, falls into hell-fire          50

    Like a bucket o' water, qush, qush.

LUSSURIOSO.                          Come,

    Be ready; nake your swords, think of your wrongs:

    This slave has injur'd you.

VINDICE.                      Troth, so he has—

    [Aside.]   And he has paid well for't.

LUSSURIOSO.

    Meet with him now.

VINDICE.                You'll bear us out, my lord?                  55

LUSSURIOSO.

    Pooh, am I a lord for nothing, think you?

    Quickly now.

VINDICE.        Sa, sa, sa, thump.            [He stabs the corpse.]

              There he lies.

---

48. beast] *Q states 1 and 2;* brest *Q*        52. nake] *Q corr., state 2;* make *Q*
(*erroneously*) *corr., state 3.*              *uncorr.* (*state 1*).
50–51.] *prose in Q.*

---

    49. *golls*] hands.        52. *nake*] make naked, unsheathe.

    55. *Meet with him*] (1) confront him in a duel; (2) requite; cf. IV.ii.122, note.

    55. *bear us out*] back us up (against any ensuing charge), be responsible for us.

    57. *Sa, sa, sa*] exclamation "formerly used by fencers when delivering a thrust" (*OED*).

LUSSURIOSO.

    Nimbly done. —Ha! O, villains, murderers,

    'Tis the old duke my father!

VINDICE.                  That's a jest.

LUSSURIOSO.

    What! stiff and cold already?                 60

    O pardon me to call you from your names;

    'Tis none of your deed. That villain Piato,

    Whom you thought now to kill, has murder'd him

    And left him thus disguis'd.

HIPPOLITO.             And not unlikely.

VINDICE.

    O rascal! Was he not asham'd              65

    To put the duke into a greasy doublet?

LUSSURIOSO.

    He has been cold and stiff, who knows how long?

VINDICE [aside].

    Marry, that do I.

LUSSURIOSO.

    No words, I pray, of anything intended.

VINDICE.

    O my lord.                        70

HIPPOLITO.

    I would fain have your lordship think that we have small

    reason to prate.

LUSSURIOSO.

    Faith, thou say'st true. I'll forthwith send to court,

    For all the nobles, bastard, duchess, all,

    How here by miracle we found him dead,      75

    And in his raiment that foul villain fled.

VINDICE.

    That will be the best way, my lord, to clear us all; let's cast

    about to be clear.

LUSSURIOSO.

    Ho, Nencio, Sordido, and the rest!

69. of] *Dodsley;* off *Q.*

---

    61. *call . . . names*] i.e., call you other than the names appropriate to your
natures.

    73. *send*] send a message.

*Enter all [his attendants].*

FIRST SERVANT.
    My lord.
SECOND SERVANT.    My lord.                                                80
LUSSURIOSO.
    Be witnesses of a strange spectacle.
    Choosing for private conference that sad room,
    We found the duke my father 'geal'd in blood.
FIRST SERVANT.
    My lord the duke!—Run, hie thee, Nencio,
    Startle the court by signifying so much.        [*Exit Nencio.*]    85
VINDICE [*aside*].
    Thus much by wit a deep revenger can:
    When murder's known, to be the clearest man.
    We're farthest off, and with as bold an eye
    Survey his body, as the standers-by.
LUSSURIOSO.
    My royal father, too basely let blood                                90
    By a malevolent slave.
HIPPOLITO [*apart to* Vindice].    Hark,
    He calls thee slave again.
VINDICE [*apart to* Hippolito].    H'as lost; he may.
LUSSURIOSO.
    O sight! Look hither, see, his lips are gnawn
    With poison.
VINDICE.                How! his lips? By th' mass, they be.
    O villain! O rogue! O slave! O rascal!                               95
HIPPOLITO [*aside*].
    O good deceit: he quits him with like terms.
FIRST [VOICE *within*].
    Where?
SECOND [VOICE *within*].    Which way?

[*Enter* Ambitioso *and* Supervacuo, *with* Nobles *and* Gentlemen.]

88. farthest] *Dodsley;* fordest *Q.*        95. O . . . rascal] *Dodsley; Q attri-*
                                            *butes line to Lussurioso.*

83. *'geal'd*] congealed.
88. *farthest off*] i.e., from suspicion.
96. *like*] i.e., doubly apt.

AMBITIOSO.

Over what roof hangs this prodigious comet
In deadly fire?

LUSSURIOSO.          Behold, behold, my lords:
the duke my father's murder'd, by a vassal that owes this     100
habit, and here left disguis'd.

[*Enter* Duchess *and* Spurio.]

DUCHESS.

My lord and husband.

SECOND NOBLE.                    Reverend majesty.

FIRST NOBLE.

I have seen these clothes often attending on him.

VINDICE [*aside*].

That nobleman has been i'th' country, for he does not lie!

SUPERVACUO [*apart to* Ambitioso].

Learn of our mother. Let's dissemble too.                     105
I am glad he's vanish'd; so I hope are you.

AMBITIOSO [*apart to* Supervacuo].

Ay, you may take my word for't.

SPURIO.                          Old dad, dead?—
[*Aside.*]   I, one of his cast sins, will send the Fates
Most hearty commendations by his own son.
I'll tug in the new stream till strength be done.             110

LUSSURIOSO.

Where be those two, that did affirm to us
My lord the duke was privately rid forth?

FIRST GENTLEMAN.

O, pardon us, my lords; he gave that charge
Upon our lives, if he were miss'd at court,
To answer so; he rode not anywhere.                          115

99. Behold . . . lords:] *prose in Q.*        113. S.P.] *Mermaid; speech assigned*
105. too] *Dodsley;* to *Q.*                  *to* 1. *(same S.P. as at l. 103)* Q.

---

98–99. *Over . . . fire*] tantamount to "Under what roof lies the evidence
of this reported disaster?" Comets of course were supposed ominous to
princes. Cf. V.iii.0.3, 23.

100. *owes*] owns.

108. *cast*] rejected, discarded; especially, set aside as disqualified (*OED*).

110. *tug*] pull with great effort; cf. Middleton, *No Wit Like a Woman's:*
"The streams of fortune, 'gainst which he tugs in vain" (*OED*).

110. *done*] complete.

We left him private with that fellow here.

VINDICE [*aside*].

Confirm'd.

LUSSURIOSO.          O heavens, that false charge was his death.

Impudent beggars! durst you to our face
Maintain such a false answer?—Bear him straight
To execution.

FIRST GENTLEMAN. My lord!

LUSSURIOSO.                    Urge me no more.          120

In this, the excuse may be call'd half the murder!

VINDICE [*aside*].

You've sentenc'd well.

LUSSURIOSO.          Away, see it be done.

                    [*Exeunt* Gentlemen, *guarded.*]

VINDICE [*aside*].

Could you not stick? See what confession doth?
Who would not lie when men are hang'd for truth?

HIPPOLITO [*apart to* Vindice].

Brother, how happy is our vengeance.

VINDICE [*apart to* Hippolito].          Why, it hits          125

Past the apprehension of indifferent wits.

LUSSURIOSO.

My lord, let post horse be sent into all
Places to entrap the villain.

VINDICE [*aside*].          Post horse! ha, ha.

FIRST NOBLE.

My lord, we're something bold to know our duty.
Your father's accidentally departed;          130
The titles that were due to him meet you.

LUSSURIOSO.

Meet me? I'm not at leisure, my good lord;
I've many griefs to dispatch out o'th' way.—
[*Aside.*]   Welcome, sweet titles. —Talk to me, my lords,
Of sepulchers and mighty emperors' bones;          135

120. S.P. FIRST GENTLEMAN] *Mermaid; speech assigned to* 1. *Q.*

---

122. *sentenc'd well*] pronounced (1) a correct opinion and (ironically)
(2) an appropriate condemnation to a punishment.
123. *stick*] (1) stand fast, or (2) stop your discourse (*OED*).

That's thought for me.

VINDICE [*aside*].          So one may see by this
How foreign markets go:
Courtiers have feet o'th' nines, and tongues o'th' twelves;
They flatter dukes and dukes flatter themselves.

SECOND NOBLE.
My lord, it is your shine must comfort us.          140

LUSSURIOSO.
Alas, I shine in tears, like the sun in April.

FIRST NOBLE.
You're now my lord's grace.

LUSSURIOSO.          My lord's grace!
I perceive you'll have it so.

FIRST NOBLE.          'Tis but your own.

LUSSURIOSO.
Then, heavens, give me grace to be so!

VINDICE [*aside*].
He prays well for himself.

SECOND NOBLE [*to the* Duchess].   Madam, all sorrows          145
Must run their circles into joys. No doubt but time
Will make the murderer bring forth himself.

VINDICE [*aside*].
He were an ass then, i'faith.

FIRST NOBLE.          In the mean season,
Let us bethink the latest funeral honors
Due to the duke's cold body; and withal,          150
Calling to memory our new happiness,
Spread in his royal son. Lords, gentlemen,
Prepare for revels.

VINDICE [*aside*].          Revels!

SECOND NOBLE.          Time hath several falls;
Griefs lift up joys, feasts put down funerals.

LUSSURIOSO.
Come then, my lords, my favors to you all.—          155

142. You're] *Dodsley;* Your *Q.*

----

138. *feet . . . twelves*] i.e., size nine feet, but flattering tongues size twelve.
152. *Spread*] extend by growth, the sense being dependent upon the pun on *son*, exploiting the sun: prince image initiated in ll. 140–141.
153. *Time . . . falls*] *falls* literally are flat collars or veils; the sense is "Time has several costumes, changes of shape."

[*Aside.*]   The duchess is suspected foully bent;
I'll begin dukedom with her banishment.

        *Exeunt* Duke [Lussurioso], Nobles, *and* Duchess.

HIPPOLITO [*apart to* Vindice].

    Revels!

VINDICE [*apart to* Hippolito].   Ay, that's the word; we are firm yet;
Strike one strain more, and then we crown our wit.

        *Exeunt Brothers* [Vindice *and* Hippolito].

SPURIO [*aside*]

    Well, have at the fairest mark—               160
So said the duke when he begot me;
And if I miss his heart or near about,
Then have at any; a bastard scorns to be out.    [*Exit* Spurio.]

SUPERVACUO.

    Not'st thou that Spurio, brother?

AMBITIOSO.

    Yes, I note him to our shame.                 165

SUPERVACUO.

    He shall not live, his hair shall not grow much longer.
In this time of revels tricks may be set afoot. Seest thou
yon new moon? It shall outlive the new duke by much;
this hand shall dispossess him, then we're mighty.
A mask is treason's license: that build upon;       170
'Tis murder's best face when a vizard's on.

                         *Exit* Supervacuo.

AMBITIOSO.

    Is't so? 't's very good;
And do you think to be duke then, kind brother?
I'll see fair play: drop one, and there lies t'other.

                         *Exit* Ambitioso.

160. at] *Dodsley; not in* Q.        165. S.P.] *And.* Q.

---

159. *Strike . . . more*] figuratively applying: play one more section (of a
piece of music).
    160. *have at*] cf. III.v.136, note.
    160. *mark*] target.
    162. *his*] presumably Lussurioso's.
    163. *to be out*] "not in the game, or in the active or leading position"
(*OED*).

[V.ii]

*Enter* Vindice *and* Hippolito, *with* Piero *and other* Lords.

VINDICE.

My lords, be all of music;
Strike old griefs into other countries
That flow in too much milk and have faint livers,
Not daring to stab home their discontents.
Let our hid flames break out, as fire, as lightning,          5
To blast this villainous dukedom vex'd with sin;
Wind up your souls to their full height again.

PIERO.

How?

FIRST LORD.    Which way?

THIRD LORD.                    Any way; our wrongs are such,
We cannot justly be reveng'd too much.

VINDICE.

You shall have all enough. Revels are toward,          10
And those few nobles that have long suppress'd you
Are busied to the furnishing of a masque,
And do affect to make a pleasant tale on't.
The masquing suits are fashioning—now comes in
That which must glad us all: we to take pattern          15
Of all those suits, the color, trimming, fashion,
E'en to an undistinguish'd hair almost.
Then, ent'ring first, observing the true form,
Within a strain or two we shall find leisure
To steal our swords out handsomely,          20
And when they think their pleasure sweet and good,
In midst of all their joys, they shall sigh blood.

PIERO.

Weightily, effectually!

13. tale] *Dodsley;* taile *Q.*

---

3. *milk*] i.e., gentleness.
3. *faint livers*] punning on *liver* as (1) inhabitant, (2) seat of the violent passions, those who *have faint livers* being cowards.
7. *Wind up*] draw up.
13. *affect*] aspire.
19. *strain*] measure.
23. *effectually*] "with the due or intended result" (Onions).

THIRD LORD.
Before the t'other masquers come—
VINDICE.
We're gone, all done and past. 25
PIERO.
But how for the duke's guard?
VINDICE.                    Let that alone;
By one and one their strengths shall be drunk down.
HIPPOLITO.
There are five hundred gentlemen in the action,
That will apply themselves, and not stand idle.
PIERO.
O, let us hug your bosoms!
VINDICE.                    Come, my lords, 30
Prepare for deeds; let other times have words.    *Exeunt.*

[V.iii]
*In a dumb show, the possessing of the young Duke, with all his Nobles; then
sounding music. A furnish'd table is brought forth; then enters the* Duke
[Lussurioso] *and his* Nobles *to the banquet. A blazing star appeareth.*

FIRST NOBLE.
Many harmonious hours and choicest pleasures
Fill up the royal numbers of your years.
LUSSURIOSO.
My lords, we're pleas'd to thank you, though we know
'Tis but your duty now to wish it so.
SECOND NOBLE.
That shine makes us all happy.
THIRD NOBLE [*aside*].            His grace frowns. 5
SECOND NOBLE [*aside*].
Yet we must say he smiles.
FIRST NOBLE [*aside*].          I think we must.

1. S.P.] *Noble. Q.*          5. S.P. SECOND NOBLE] *Harrier; Nob.
Q.*

24. *the t'other*] a frequent vulgarism for "the other."
[V.iii]
    0.1. *possessing*] putting in possession, coronation.
    0.2. *sounding*] loud, sonorous.
    0.3. *A blazing star*] a comet; cf. V.i.98–99.

LUSSURIOSO [*aside*].

    That foul-incontinent duchess we have banish'd;

    The bastard shall not live. After these revels,

    I'll begin strange ones; he and the stepsons

    Shall pay their lives for the first subsidies.        10

    We must not frown so soon, else 'tad been now.

FIRST NOBLE.

    My gracious lord, please you prepare for pleasure;

    The masque is not far off.

LUSSURIOSO.                   We are for pleasure—

    [*To the star.*]   Beshrew thee! what art thou?—Mad'st me start?

    Thou hast committed treason. —A blazing star!     15

FIRST NOBLE.

    A blazing star, O where, my lord?

LUSSURIOSO.                   Spy out.

SECOND NOBLE.

    See, see, my lords, a wondrous-dreadful one!

LUSSURIOSO.

    I am not pleas'd at that ill-knotted fire,

    That bushing-flaring star. Am not I duke?

    It should not quake me now; had it appear'd     20

    Before it, I might then have justly fear'd.

    But yet they say, whom art and learning weds,

    When stars wear locks, they threaten great men's heads.

    Is it so? You are read, my lords.

FIRST NOBLE.               May it please your grace,

    It shows great anger.

LUSSURIOSO.            That does not please our grace.     25

SECOND NOBLE.

    Yet here's the comfort, my lord: many times,

    When it seemes most, it threatens farthest off.

---

23. wear] *Dodsley;* were *Q.*

---

10. *subsidies*] "a pecuniary aid exacted by a prince," particularly, in England, "aid granted by parliament to the sovereign to meet special needs" (*OED*).

21. *it*] i.e., my becoming duke.

23. *When . . . locks*] i.e., when they are comets.

27. *seemes most*] is most in view, most (immediately) manifest; *seemes* is disyllabic.

LUSSURIOSO.
    Faith, and I think so too.
FIRST NOBLE.                Beside, my lord,
    You're gracefully establish'd with the loves
    Of all your subjects; and for natural death,          30
    I hope it will be threescore years a-coming.
LUSSURIOSO.
    True; no more but threescore years?
FIRST NOBLE.
    Fourscore, I hope, my lord.
SECOND NOBLE.               And fivescore, I.
THIRD NOBLE.
    But 'tis my hope, my lord, you shall ne'er die.
LUSSURIOSO.
    Give me thy hand, these others I rebuke;         35
    He that hopes so is fittest for a duke.
    Thou shalt sit next me. —Take your places, lords;
    We're ready now for sports; let 'em set on.—
    You thing! we shall forget you quite anon!
THIRD NOBLE.
    I hear 'em coming, my lord.

*Enter the masque of revengers: the two brothers* [Vindice *and* Hippolito], *and two Lords more.*

LUSSURIOSO.               Ah, 'tis well.—         40
    [*Aside.*] Brothers, and bastard, you dance next in hell.

*The revengers dance; at the end,* [*they*] *steal out their swords, and these four kill the four at the table, in their chairs. It thunders.*

VINDICE.
    Mark, thunder!
    Dost know thy cue, thou big-voic'd crier?
    Dukes' groans are thunder's watchwords.
HIPPOLITO.
    So, my lords, you have enough.         45

40. S.D.] *Q prints in margin beside*    43. big-voic'd] *Reed;* big-voyc'st *Q.*
*ll. 40–41.*

---

44 *watchwords.*] preconcerted signals to begin an attack (*OED*).

VINDICE.

Come, let's away, no ling'ring.

HIPPOLITO.                              Follow!—[*To the* Lords.]—Go!

*Exeunt [revengers except* Vindice].

VINDICE.

No power is angry when the lustful die;
When thunder claps, heaven likes the tragedy.          *Exit* Vindice.

*Enter the other masque of intended murderers: Stepsons* [Ambitioso *and*
Supervacuo], *Bastard* [Spurio], *and a* Fourth Lord, *coming in dancing.
The Duke* [Lussurioso] *recovers a little in voice, and groans;* [*he*] *calls,
"A guard, treason." At which they all start out of their measure, and turning
towards the table, they find them all to be murdered.*

LUSSURIOSO.

O, O.

SPURIO.          Whose groan was that?

LUSSURIOSO.                              Treason, a guard.

AMBITIOSO.

How now? All murder'd!

SUPERVACUO.                    Murder'd!                              50

FOURTH LORD.

And those his nobles!

AMBITIOSO.                    Here's a labor sav'd;

I thought to have sped him. 'Sblood, how came this?

SUPERVACUO.

Then I proclaim myself; now I am duke.

AMBITIOSO.

Thou duke! brother, thou liest.          [*He slays* Supervacuo.]

SPURIO.                              Slave, so dost thou.

[*He slays* Ambitioso.]

FOURTH LORD.

Base villain, hast thou slain my lord and master?          55

[*He slays* Spurio.]

[*Re-*]*enter the first men* [Vindice, Hippolito, *and the two Lords*].

46.1] *after* lingring. *Q.*                    53. S.P.] *Napier conj.; speech assigned
48.1–5] *after* Oh, oh. (*l. 49*) *Q.*          to Spur. *Q.*
48.2. Lord] *Mermaid; man* Q.                   55. S.P.] 4. *Q.*

48.4. *measure*] dance.

VINDICE.

    Pistols! treason! murder! help! Guard my lord

    The duke!

                [*Enter* Antonio *and the guard.*]

HIPPOLITO.    Lay hold upon this traitor!

                      [*They seize* Fourth Lord.]

LUSSURIOSO.               O.

VINDICE.

    Alas, the duke is murder'd!

HIPPOLITO.           And the nobles.

VINDICE.

    Surgeons, surgeons!— [*Aside.*]   Heart! does he breathe so long?

ANTONIO.

    A piteous tragedy! able to wake              60

    An old man's eyes bloodshot.

LUSSURIOSO.         O.

VINDICE.             Look to my lord

    The duke. —[*Aside.*]   A vengeance throttle him.—

    [*To* Fourth Lord.]   Confess, thou murd'rous and unhallowed

      man,

    Didst thou kill all these?

FOURTH LORD.      None but the bastard, I.

VINDICE.

    How came the duke slain, then?

FOURTH LORD.      We found him so.        65

LUSSURIOSO.

    O villain.

VINDICE.    Hark.

LUSSURIOSO.    Those in the masque did murder us.

VINDICE.

    Law you now, sir.

    O marble impudence! will you confess now?

FOURTH LORD.

    'Slud, 'tis all false!

57. traitor] *Collins;* Traytors *Q.*    69. 'Slud] *Collins;* Sloud *Q.*
63. unhallowed] *Dodsley;* vnhol-
lowed *Q.*

---

67. *Law you*] an asseverative exclamation.

ANTONIO.                    Away with that foul monster,

  Dipp'd in a prince's blood.

FOURTH LORD.                    Heart, 'tis a lie!                    70

ANTONIO.

  Let him have bitter execution.

                    [*Exit Guard with* Fourth Lord.]

VINDICE [*aside*].

  New marrow! No, I cannot be express'd.—

  How fares my lord, the duke?

LUSSURIOSO.                    Farewell to all;

  He that climbs highest has the greatest fall.

  My tongue is out of office.

VINDICE.                    Air, gentlemen, air!—                    75

                    [*The others step back.*]

  [*Whispers to* Lussurioso.]   Now thou'lt not prate on't, 'twas

      Vindice murder'd thee—

LUSSURIOSO.

  O.

VINDICE [*whispers*].   Murder'd thy father—

LUSSURIOSO.                    O.

VINDICE [*whispers*].                    —And I am he.

                    [Lussurioso *dies.*]

  Tell nobody. —[*Aloud.*]   So, so, the duke's departed.

ANTONIO.

  It was a deadly hand that wounded him;

  The rest, ambitious who should rule and sway                    80

  After his death, were so made all away.

VINDICE.

  My lord was unlikely.

HIPPOLITO [*to* Antonio].   Now the hope

  Of Italy lies in your reverend years.

VINDICE.

  Your hair will make the silver age again,

73. fares] *Dodsley;* faires *Q.*        80–81. sway/ . . . death,] *Dodsley;*
                                         sway,/ . . . death *Q.*

---

72. *New marrow*] Nicoll takes this self-congratulatory exclamation to
mean "New food for my vengeance." Possibly *marrow* refers not only to the
delicacy but (ironically, and preparatively) to this further "'goodness' of"
(*OED*) or extracted by his vengeful plot.

  82. *unlikely*] unpromising.

When there was fewer but more honest men.                    85

ANTONIO.

The burden's weighty and will press age down.

May I so rule that heaven may keep the crown.

VINDICE.

The rape of your good lady has been 'quited,

With death on death.

ANTONIO.                              Just is the law above.

But of all things it puts me most to wonder            90

How the old duke came murder'd.

VINDICE.                                  O, my lord.

ANTONIO.

It was the strangeliest carried; I've not heard

Of the like.

HIPPOLITO.        'Twas all done for the best, my lord.

VINDICE.

All for your grace's good.

We may be bold to speak it now.                    95

'Twas somewhat witty carried though we say it:

'Twas we two murder'd him.

ANTONIO.                          You two?

VINDICE.

None else, i'faith, my lord; nay, 'twas well manag'd.

ANTONIO.

Lay hands upon those villains.        [*Guards seize them.*]

VINDICE.                          How! on us?

ANTONIO.

Bear 'em to speedy execution.                    100

VINDICE.

Heart! was't not for your good, my lord?

ANTONIO.

My good!—Away with 'em. —Such an old man as he!

You, that would murder him, would murder me!

VINDICE.

Is't come about?

87. may] *Dodsley;* nay *Q.*              hard *Q.*
92. I've not heard] *Dodsley;* I not    100. to] *Dodsley;* two *Q.*

---

104. *come about*] in both obvious senses.

HIPPOLITO.                'Sfoot, brother, you begun.

VINDICE.

May not we set as well as the duke's son?                    105
Thou hast no conscience: are we not reveng'd?
Is there one enemy left alive amongst those?
'Tis time to die, when we are ourselves our foes.
When murd'rers shut deeds close, this curse does seal 'em:
If none disclose 'em, they themselves reveal 'em!          110
This murder might have slept in tongueless brass,
But for ourselves, and the world died an ass.
Now I remember too, here was Piato
Brought forth a knavish sentence once;
No doubt (said he) but time                                  115
Will make the murderer bring forth himself.
'Tis well he died; he was a witch.—
And now, my lord, since we are in forever:
This work was ours, which else might have been slipp'd;
And if we list, we could have nobles clipp'd                 120
And go for less than beggars; but we hate
To bleed so cowardly. We have enough,
I'faith, we're well: our mother turn'd, our sister true,
We die after a nest of dukes—adieu.
                    *Exeunt* [Vindice *and* Hippolito, *guarded*].

109. murd'rers] *Dodsley* (murderers); murders *Q*.

---

105. *set*] i.e., die (again playing, of course, on son:sun).
105. *duke's*] disyllabic; cf. I.i.28, note.
106. *conscience*] registering ironic awareness of the contradictions, in the
present context, among the various senses: (1) consciousness, conviction,
(2) reasonableness, (3) sense of right and wrong.
117. *witch*] because he could prophesy.
118. *are in*] "engaged, involved, entangled in (an action, esp[ecially]
an unlawful one)" (*OED*).
119. *slipp'd*] neglected.
120. *nobles clipp'd*] punning on *nobles* in the senses, (1) noblemen, (2)
the gold coins worth eight shillings, sixpence. To *clip* the latter would be
"to mutilate [them] by fraudulently paring the edge" (*OED*)—thus the
revengers would *go* less beggarly but *bleed* for a more cowardly crime.
To *have clipp'd* the former would have been to have (1) embraced, or
perhaps, (2) named (with pun on *clipped/ycleped*) *nobles*.
123. *turn'd*] i.e., in the spiritual sense, "converted toward God."

ANTONIO.

How subtly was that murder 'clos'd! Bear up                    125
Those tragic bodies; 'tis a heavy season.
Pray heaven their blood may wash away all treason.    [*Exeunt.*]

## FINIS

127. S.D.] *Exit. Q.*

125. *'clos'd*] disclosed.
126. *heavy*] sorrowful.

# Appendix

## Chronology

Approximate years are indicated by *, occurrences in doubt by ( ? ).

| *Political and Literary Events* | *Life and Major Works of Tourneur* |
|---|---|
| **1558**<br>Accession of Queen Elizabeth I.<br>Robert Greene born.<br>Thomas Kyd born. | |
| **1560**<br>George Chapman born. | |
| **1561**<br>Francis Bacon born. | |
| **1564**<br>Shakespeare born.<br>Christopher Marlowe born. | |
| **1570**<br>Thomas Heywood born.* | |
| **1572**<br>Thomas Dekker born.*<br>John Donne born.<br>Massacre of St. Bartholomew's Day. | |
| **1573**<br>Ben Jonson born.* | |
| **1576**<br>The Theatre, the first permanent public theater in London, established by James Burbage.<br>John Marston born. | |
| **1577**<br>The Curtain theater opened.<br>Holinshed's *Chronicles of England, Scotland and Ireland.* | |

Drake begins circumnavigation of
the earth; completed 1580.

1578
John Lyly's *Euphues: The Anatomy
of Wit.*

1579
John Fletcher born.
Sir Thomas North's translation of
Plutarch's *Lives.*

1580
Thomas Middleton born.

Cyril Tourneur born* (no evidence
supports the date which is thus mere
guesswork).

1583
Philip Massinger born.

1584
Francis Beaumont born.*

1586
Death of Sir Philip Sidney.
John Ford born.

1587
The Rose theater opened by Hens-
lowe.
Marlowe's *TAMBURLAINE*, Part
I.*
Execution of Mary, Queen of Scots.
Drake raids Cadiz.

1588
Defeat of the Spanish Armada.
Marlowe's *TAMBURLAINE*, Part
II.*

1589
Greene's *FRIAR BACON AND
FRIAR BUNGAY.*
Marlowe's *THE JEW OF
MALTA.*
Kyd's *THE SPANISH TRAGEDY.*

1590
Spenser's *Faerie Queene* (Books I–III)
published.
Sidney's *Arcadia* published.

Shakespeare's *HENRY VI*, Parts
I–III,* *TITUS ANDRONICUS.*
1591
Shakespeare's *RICHARD III.**
1592
Marlowe's *DOCTOR FAUSTUS**
and *EDWARD II.**
Shakespeare's *TAMING OF THE
SHREW** and *THE COMEDY OF
ERRORS.**
Death of Greene.
1593
Shakespeare's *LOVE'S LABOR'S
LOST*;* *Venus and Adonis* published.
Death of Marlowe.
Theaters closed on account of
plague.
1594
Shakespeare's *TWO GENTLE-
MEN OF VERONA*;* *The Rape of
Lucrece* published.
Shakespeare's company becomes
Lord Chamberlain's Men.
Death of Kyd.
1595
The Swan theater built.
Sidney's *Defense of Poesy* published.
Shakespeare's *ROMEO AND
JULIET,* *A MIDSUMMER
NIGHT'S DREAM,* *RICHARD
II.**
Raleigh's first expedition to Guiana.
1596
Spenser's *Faerie Queene* (Books IV–
VI) published.
Shakespeare's *MERCHANT OF
VENICE,* *KING JOHN.**
James Shirley born.
1597
Bacon's *Essays* (first edition).
Shakespeare's *HENRY IV*, Part I.*
1598
Demolition of The Theatre.

Shakespeare's *MUCH ADO ABOUT NOTHING,* *HENRY IV*, Part II.*
Jonson's *EVERY MAN IN HIS HUMOR* (first version).
Seven books of Chapman's translation of Homer's *Iliad* published.

1599

The Paul's Boys reopen their theater.
The Globe theater opened.
Shakespeare's *AS YOU LIKE IT,* *HENRY V*, *JULIUS CAESAR.*
Marston's *ANTONIO AND MELLIDA,* Parts I and II.
Dekker's *THE SHOEMAKERS' HOLIDAY.*
Death of Spenser.

1600

Shakespeare's *TWELFTH NIGHT.*
The Fortune theater built by Alleyn.
The Children of the Chapel begin to play at the Blackfriars.

Publishes a satiric verse allegory, *The Transformed Metamorphosis.*

1601

Shakespeare's *HAMLET,* *MERRY WIVES OF WINDSOR.*
Insurrection and execution of the Earl of Essex.
Jonson's *POETASTER.*

1602

Shakespeare's *TROILUS AND CRESSIDA.*

1603

Death of Queen Elizabeth I; accession of James VI of Scotland as James I.
Florio's translation of Montaigne's *Essays* published.
Shakespeare's *ALL'S WELL THAT ENDS WELL.*
Heywood's *A WOMAN KILLED WITH KINDNESS.*
Marston's *THE MALCONTENT.*

Shakespeare's company becomes
the King's Men.

1604

Shakespeare's *MEASURE FOR
MEASURE,*\* *OTHELLO.*\*
Marston's *THE FAWN.*\*
Chapman's *BUSSY D'AMBOIS.*\*

1605

Shakespeare's *KING LEAR.*\*
Marston's *THE DUTCH COURTE-
SAN.*\*
Bacon's *Advancement of Learning* pub-
lished.
The Gunpowder Plot.

*Laugh and lie down: or, The world's
Folly,* a satiric prose pamphlet,
(with dedication) signed C. T.,
sometimes attributed to Tourneur,
published.

1606

Shakespeare's *MACBETH.*\*
Jonson's *VOLPONE.*\*
The Red Bull theater built.
Death of John Lyly.

*THE REVENGER'S TRAGEDY*
(King's Men).\*

1607

Shakespeare's *ANTONY AND
CLEOPATRA.*\*
Beaumont's *KNIGHT OF THE
BURNING PESTLE.*\*
Settlement of Jamestown, Virginia.

*THE REVENGER'S TRAGEDY*
published (without ascription of
authorship).

1608

Shakespeare's *CORIOLANUS,*\*
*TIMON OF ATHENS,*\* *PERI-
CLES.*\*
Chapman's *CONSPIRACY AND
TRAGEDY OF CHARLES, DUKE
OF BYRON.*\*
Dekker's *Gull's Hornbook* published.
Richard Burbage leases Blackfriars
Theatre for King's Company.
John Milton born.

1609

Shakespeare's *CYMBELINE;*\*
*Sonnets* published.
Jonson's *EPICOENE.*

Publishes *A Funeral Poem upon the
Death of the Most Worthy and True
Soldier, Sir Francis Vere* (who had
died August 28, 1608).

1610

Jonson's *ALCHEMIST.*
Chapman's *REVENGE OF BUSSY D'AMBOIS.* *
Richard Crashaw born.

*THE ATHEIST'S TRAGEDY.* *

1611

Authorized (King James) Version of the Bible published.
Shakespeare's *THE WINTER'S TALE,* * *THE TEMPEST.* *
Beaumont and Fletcher's *A KING AND NO KING.*
Middleton's *A CHASTE MAID IN CHEAPSIDE.*
Chapman's translation of *Iliad* completed.

*THE ATHEIST'S TRAGEDY* published.

1612

Webster's *THE WHITE DEVIL.* *

Tourneur's tragicomedy, *THE NOBLEMAN* (now lost), entered in Stationers' Register, and performed at Court February 23 and during Christmas. Writes *The Character of Robert Earl of Salisbury* * (first printed, as Tourneur's, by Nicoll, 1929), and *A Grief On the Death of Prince Henry* (who had died November 6).

1613

The Globe theater burned.
Shakespeare's *HENRY VIII* (with Fletcher).
Webster's *THE DUCHESS OF MALFI.* *
Sir Thomas Overbury murdered.

*A Grief on the Death of Prince Henry* published, with elegies by Webster and Heywood, in *Three Elegies*. Robert Daborne writes Philip Henslowe, June 5, that he had given Tourneur an act of *THE ARRAIGNMENT OF LONDON* (not extant) to write. Tourneur granted 40 shillings, December 23, on warrant of the Lord Chamberlain, for letters carried from London to Brussels.

1614

The Globe theater rebuilt.
The Hope Theatre built.
Jonson's *BARTHOLOMEW FAIR.*

Has annual pension of £60 from the United Provinces. *

**1616**
Publication of Folio edition of Jonson's *Works*.
Chapman's *Whole Works of Homer*.
Death of Shakespeare.
Death of Beaumont.

**1617**

Arrested (for cause now unknown) on a warrant issued by the Privy Council September 1. Released October 18 on bond, taken of Sir Edward Cecil, that he would "at all times" appear when summoned.

**1618**
Outbreak of Thirty Years War.
Execution of Raleigh.

**1620**
Settlement of Plymouth, Massachusetts.

**1621**
Middleton's *WOMEN BEWARE WOMEN.*\*
Robert Burton's *Anatomy of Melancholy* published.
Andrew Marvell born.

**1622**
Middleton and Rowley's *THE CHANGELING.*\*
Henry Vaughan born.

**1623**
Publication of Folio edition of Shakespeare's *COMEDIES, HISTORIES, AND TRAGEDIES.*

**1625**
Death of King James I; accession of Charles I.
Death of Fletcher.

Serves as Secretary to the Council of War from August 2 to September 26. In the post of Secretary to the Marshal's Court, sails with the expedition against Cadiz (Sir Edward Cecil, Lord Marshal) from Plymouth, October 8. Tourneur among the deathly ill put off at the port of Kinsale, Ireland, December 11, at the fleet's return.

**1626**
Death of Bacon.

Tourneur dies in Ireland, February 28.

**1627**
Death of Middleton.

**1628**
Ford's *THE LOVER'S MELAN-CHOLY*.
Petition of Right.
Buckingham assassinated.

**1631**
Shirley's *THE TRAITOR*.
Death of Donne.
John Dryden born.

**1632**
Massinger's *THE CITY MADAM.**

Tourneur's widow, Mary, renewing her petition to the Council of War for his pay as Secretary to the Council, claims his death left her "destitute of all means of livelihood."

**1633**
Donne's *Poems* published.
Death of George Herbert.

**1634**
Death of Chapman, Marston, Webster.*
Publication of *THE TWO NOBLE KINSMEN*, with title-page attribution to Shakespeare and Fletcher.
Milton's *Comus*.

**1635**
Sir Thomas Browne's *Religio Medici*.

**1637**
Death of Jonson.

**1639**
First Bishops' War.
Death of Carew.*

**1640**
Short Parliament.
Long Parliament impeaches Laud.
Death of Massinger, Burton.

1641
Irish rebel.
Death of Heywood.

1642
Charles I leaves London; Civil War
breaks out.
Shirley's *COURT SECRET*.
All theaters closed by Act of Parlia-
ment.

1643
Parliament swears to the Solemn
League and Covenant.

1645
Ordinance for New Model Army
enacted.

1646
End of First Civil War.

1647
Army occupies London.
Charles I forms alliance with
Scots.
Publication of Folio edition of
Beaumount and Fletcher's *COM-
EDIES AND TRAGEDIES*.

1648
Second Civil War.

1649
Execution of Charles I.

1650
Jeremy Collier born.

1651
Hobbes' *Leviathan* published.

1652
First Dutch War began (ended
1654).
Thomas Otway born.

1653
Nathaniel Lee born.*

1656
D'Avenant's *THE SIEGE OF
RHODES* performed at Rutland
House.

1657
John Dennis born.
1658
Death of Oliver Cromwell.
D'Avenant's *THE CRUELTY OF THE SPANIARDS IN PERU* performed at the Cockpit.
1660
Restoration of Charles II.
Theatrical patents granted to Thomas Killigrew and Sir William D'Avenant, authorizing them to form, respectively, the King's and the Duke of York's Companies.
1661
Cowley's *THE CUTTER OF COLEMAN STREET.*
D'Avenant's *THE SIEGE OF RHODES* expanded to two parts.
1662
Charter granted to the Royal Society.
1663
Dryden's *THE WILD GALLANT.*
Tuke's *THE ADVENTURES OF FIVE HOURS.*
1664
Sir John Vanbrugh born.
Dryden's *THE RIVAL LADIES.*
Dryden and Howard's *THE INDIAN QUEEN.*
Etherege's *THE COMICAL REVENGE.*
1665
Second Dutch War began (ended 1667).
Great Plague.
Dryden's *THE INDIAN EMPEROR.*
Orrery's *MUSTAPHA.*
1666
Fire of London.
Death of James Shirley.